Dreaming of Dante

Dreaming of Dante

A SPIRITUAL JOURNEY FROM A SCIENTIST'S PERSPECTIVE

Mario Canki, PhD

Dreaming of Dante: A Spiritual Journey from a Scientist's Perspective

Subjects: Awareness. | Higher Self. |Meditation. | Spirituality. | Brain - Neurophysiology.

First paperback edition: February 2026

ISBN 979-8-9940985-0-9 (paperback)

Book design by Duane Stapp

Published in the United States of America by Brookhaven Press

For permissions and inquiries, contact:
www.mariocanki.com

Table of Contents

List of Illustrations

For Nanette

my teacher and friend

Foreword

We are in the midst of a profound shift in how people seek answers to the deep anxieties that come with being human. The old, codified responses from organized religion often fail to hold up against the raw and repetitive suffering we now witness in real time through a twenty-four-hour news cycle.

Many people—especially young adults—no longer identify with any traditional religious group. Often referred to as the "Nones," they are *not* rejecting meaning or purpose. Instead, they are searching for approaches that are personal, experiential, and grounded in direct understanding rather than dogma. They want practices that can be verified in their own lives and that help them meet the challenges of today's world with clarity and compassion.

Dr. Canki's book offers an invaluable starting point for this kind of search. His reflections speak to the doubts and discoveries that arise for anyone exploring the deeper dimensions of life. By telling his story with honesty and vulnerability, he provides readers with a mirror for their own journeys. His descriptions remind us that awakening does not happen in abstraction, but amid our daily struggles, relationships, and questions.

This form of storytelling has a long lineage. Dante's *Divine Comedy*, written in the fourteenth century, opens not with lofty theory but with Dante himself—lost, despairing, and exiled. His journey takes him through confusion and darkness toward insight and peace. Dr. Canki, in his own way, walks a similar path, showing how moments of crisis and disorientation can become gateways to understanding.

At a time when so many are seeking new ways to make sense of life's challenges, *Dreaming of Dante* arrives as a guide and companion. I highly recommend it to anyone who senses there is more to life and is ready to embark on a journey of discovery, starting exactly where they are.

Richard Schaub, PhD
Author of *The End of Fear: A Spiritual Path for Realists*

Author's Note

This book is a work of my memory and personal reflection. While I've done my best to recount events and conversations as accurately as possible, certain names, identifying details, and sequences of events have been changed to protect privacy and to preserve the flow of the story.

The experiences I share here are my own. They are not intended as medical advice and should never replace the care or guidance of a qualified healthcare professional. If you have questions or concerns about your physical or mental health, please seek professional support.

I've made every effort to acknowledge and credit all quotations and sources included in this book. Excerpts from *Dante: The Divine Comedy. Volume I: Inferno, Volume II: Purgatory, Volume III: Paradise,* translated by Mark Musa, used by permission of Indiana University Press.

Any errors or omissions are entirely unintentional, and I welcome corrections for future editions.

Preface

All the life mysteries are contained within us, hidden in the deep recesses of our minds and hearts. In fact, our individual inner wisdom is what, throughout millennia, has been referred to as our higher self.

The labor of spiritual discovery is what the great Italian poet and philosopher Dante Alighieri described in his *Divine Comedy*. Inspired by his ultimate mountain climb toward union with a higher self, I sought to follow that path too. By illuminating the convergence of my own worldly and spiritual experiences, I aspire to provide guidance for the seeker in you, because you too can do this, and I hope that these pages guide you toward that goal.

Introduction

The last scientific publication of my career—"Use of *Sargassum fusiforme* Extract and its Bioactive Molecules to Inhibit HIV Infection"[1]—is on bridging the Eastern and Western paradigms of healing: merging the traditional Eastern approach of looking at the human body holistically with the Western approach of one-pointed focus on a specific illness.

In this book, I am building a bridge as well: one that connects the millennia-old tenets of Buddhism and Hinduism with the much more recent—but no less profound—philosophical insights of Western culture. A bridge between the metaphysical origins of the spiritual experience, and the emergent scientific understanding of the mechanics of it. A bridge between esoteric knowledge, and rational understanding.

This book is meant for the seeker in you—who, like the Pilgrim in Dante Alighieri's *Divine Comedy*—is climbing the spiritual mountain toward the ultimate union with his higher self, his Beatrice. The labor of this journey, but, more importantly, the roadmap of the spiritual realm it takes place in, is what Dante describes in his *Divine Comedy*. This mountain path is meant for all those who are searching for greater comprehension and for a first-hand experience of life's mysteries—be it through yogic practice, Buddhist contemplation, or the divine mysticism of Dante's spiritual quest.

The *Divine Comedy* is an epic poem that consists of three parts, each corresponding to a distinct level of spiritual evolution that the seeker must traverse. It begins with the Hell of human suffering, moves through the Purgatory process of transmutation, and ends in the mysticism of Paradise. Dante wrote this poem as a guide to help people uncover their inner wisdom—their higher self, and experiences of unity. It was meant as a roadmap for humanity to alleviate its daily miseries and unhappiness. In many ways, Dante's poem mirrors his spiritual journey, extracting himself from the depths of Hell, through the upward striving of the realm of Purgatory, to the ultimate mystical experience of oneness with Universal energies of light, unity, and love.

Like every student on the spiritual path to enlightenment who has chosen to follow a guide—a guru, or a teacher—the Pilgrim is helped along the way by the poet Virgil, who represents reason and guides him through the human experience of Hell and Purgatory. Virgil shows the Pilgrim the worst sins and worldly risks to one's soul, but also guides him on the path that leads out of these realms, toward the nirvana of Paradise.

If you want to realize your inner power, to unlock your own metaphysical secrets, or simply reconcile moral and existential ambiguity, you are not alone, and these pages are meant for you. If you have deeper questions about the purpose and meaning of life, this book can help. Here, I offer my experiences at the intersection of the day-to-day and spiritual as a roadmap for the seeker.

At times, with much anguish, I have wrestled to reconcile the two sides of the coin—the mundane and the spiritual. The Buddhist Middle Way eluded me often. Pursuing the spiritual direction was satisfying, but I had deeper questions and needed to understand the scientific basis behind my experiences. My ambition was to unite these two sides into one, a balanced expression of my personality. I needed to understand the point of intersection between science and spirit, and I wanted to merge the mind and the heart into a meaningful and practical life, filled with purpose and meaning. Unsatisfied with my existence, I changed the mundane trajectory of my life toward a career in science, and at the same time enthusiastically pursued inner spiritual mysteries. Synthesizing the ordinary with the extraordinary turned out to be my own Middle Way. This has given me some of the happiest moments of my life.

I studied the teaching of Higher Self Yoga developed by Nanette V. Hucknall for over forty years and along the way was inspired by Dante. Merging esoteric knowledge with emerging scientific evidence that explains the phenomena the Pilgrim encountered in contemporary terms, I incorporated Dante's model for the seeker with my own knowledge of the higher self to explain the spiritual quest through scientific studies that clarify many metaphysical concepts. I conceptualize these ideas into what I teach today to students and seekers on the path of self-discovery.

My own journey started from deep despair and unhappiness. I was lost but always knew that destiny was waiting for me. Lack of purpose and meaning propelled me on the path of self-discovery. Now, a scientist and a teacher of spiritual yoga, I do believe a life in service of humankind is—in the Buddhist sense—the only way to find true happiness and meaning. And the best service is teaching skills to others for the practice of self-discovery that will guide their life's purpose.

This book is meant for the seeker in you, for all those who are searching for greater comprehension and a first-hand experience of life's mysteries—be it through yogic practice or the divine mysticism of Dante's personal and mystical quest.

Part 1: BECOMING

Midway along the journey of our life
I woke to find myself in a dark wood,
for I had wandered off from the straight path.

Dante (*Inferno*, Canto I, 1-3)

THE DISCONTENT

At the age of forty-one, Dante Alighieri found himself in midlife crisis. Already a celebrated poet, he was a political exile from his beloved home city of Florence, living at the mercy of a string of wealthy admirers of his art. He had already experienced the ups and downs of life, only to find himself lost and bewildered in the dark woods of uncertainty and self-doubt.

My discontent began much earlier, in my teens, and over the years, it built up to tremendous boredom, unhappiness, and general despair. As a child and adolescent growing up in Croatia, I had a deep-seated—albeit nebulous—desire to make a positive impact in the world. I had a sense there was a destiny I was meant to fulfill—not necessarily anything grandiose, but something meaningful that would give me purpose. I was unsure what that might be. This calling stayed with me throughout my adolescence. Early on at school, I often daydreamed, looking out of the large windows, enjoying the sun reflecting on the leaves of the old chestnut trees growing in the schoolyard. When the teacher called on me, jolting me out of my pleasant reverie, I had no idea what the question was. Embarrassing!

After my parents' divorce when I was sixteen years old, I arrived in New York City with my mother. The process of adapting to the physical and emotional changes of a new continent and culture was arduous and overwhelming. The city's unconventional architecture—with its strange, wrought-iron fire escapes—was unfamiliar, and the new language was a challenge to learn. It was a significant contrast to my comfortable European lifestyle, friends, and traditions. I was homesick and lost. The morning after our arrival, the relatives we stayed with offered us lunch: peanut butter and jelly sandwiches. I remember holding back tears over the slice of white bread, it was so alien and weird.

These were difficult and confusing times for an uprooted teenager. I was lost and often embarrassed by my poor English, but luckily there were plenty of understanding girls interested in my European roots, which soothed my teenage angst. Nonetheless, I yearned for my old city—for the familiar streets and the comforting smells. In the summers, I returned home, visiting friends I'd left behind. Eventually I came to the painful realization that I could not mentally be in two places at once. This uncomfortable transition period had to end, and it was time to sever the connection to the old, and to fully embrace my new country with all of its unique lessons and opportunities. I made a decision and stopped going back home, and with time my feeling of loss lessened and eventually faded from my memory.

After graduating high school, I studied business administration in college, mostly because I did not have a firm idea of what to do with myself, not because I was drawn to it. I realized very quickly that I lacked motivation and a clear sense of direction. Studying corporate law was superficially interesting, as it challenged my intellect and provoked rational thinking, but accounting and management were a chore, boring beyond words. Clearly not for me.

By chance I got a camera and found passion for photography, and even received recognition for my artistic skills, winning several local awards—it was an outlet for creativity and a source of fulfillment. I studied with a local photographer: composition and darkroom techniques, which fulfilled my artistic side—but intellectual engagement was still lacking.

In my early twenties, I thought of heading for California—to start a new life, study photography, and make it big in art circles. Since I was quite broke and unable to finance this life plan, I ended up stuck in New York City without resources or a clear vision for my future—and instead landed a position with an international bank on Wall Street. I managed the back office for foreign exchange trading, which consisted of a dozen or so people. My job was to ensure all currency trades were paid by closing time each day. Although I had responsibilities and managed others, and even got married, I still wandered without a sense of purpose. It felt as if I were sacrificing my values for a paycheck, and it wasn't making me happy—far from it. While my wife was ready to move to the suburbs and start a family, I grew jittery and dissatisfied, even frightened. That's how that marriage fell apart.

At the bank, I befriended some of the guys making the currency trades. They partied hard to relieve the stress of the high-stakes job, which involved making—and sometimes losing—significant amounts of money. They would get free tickets to sold-out sporting events and other forms of entertainment, and I joined in the fun. Basketball games at Madison Square Garden were enjoyable, especially the courtside seats. However, I soon realized this was just a way to escape the daily routine, the tedium of trading, and the endless pursuit of making ever more money. I also realized that this kind of capitalism was not for me; it all seemed meaningless and left me feeling empty inside.

Having to wear a suit and a tie did not help. Neither did commuting to work on a packed subway with fellow travelers reading the *New York Times,* the *Wall Street Journal,* or the *Financial Times*—the obligatory papers of the trade. This was not my crowd; I felt isolated and alone. As I exited the subway, there was always someone standing on a corner begging for change to buy a cup of coffee or something to eat. What better place to beg for a bit of change than on Wall Street, crossroads where the poor and neglected mixed with the best of the capitalist free-market economy, benefiting all. Entering my office, I needed lots of coffee and a couple of hours to regain my sense of self. It was time to reenter the matrix and do my job.

Some days were better, as I was friends with a colleague with whom I enjoyed taking long lunches to chat and commiserate. He was a vice president at the bank, and being his friend, my long lunches were tolerated—although my direct supervisor grew quite resentful. I didn't really care; what could they do, fire me? My friend and I would stroll around Battery Park, walk along the Hudson River, and at times venture even as far as Chinatown to my friend's favorite restaurant for the Peking duck special. That was quite a long walk for lunch, but worth it.

These walks relieved the daily grind and shortened the days of boredom. During our conversations, we discussed topics like existentialism, spirituality, and the meaning of life. My friend was more of an existentialist, and it was a pleasure speaking with him—as, for some reason, we seemed to be on the same mental wavelength. Originally, he was from the Caribbean, had a successful career, and yet he was conflicted about the dichotomy between the rich society he was serving and the poor nation he came from. For him, the contrast was striking, and the unresolved internal conflict, painful. We shared different yet similar dissatisfactions—but in contrast to me, he accepted his destiny, whereas I kept searching for mine. He encouraged me to return to college and get a master's degree in business so that I could advance to a higher position in the bank and make more money, but that path did not resonate with me whatsoever.

Still, I continued to run away from New York City each weekend, doing nature photography, and during the week snuck in a film roll of street photography here and there. Eventually, an opportunity presented itself to do professional studio photoshoots part-time while keeping my day job. I photographed various products to be featured in catalogs and newspaper ads, even in the *New York Times.* I became especially proficient in showcasing leather goods. The extra income was welcome, and I contemplated leaving my day job to build a full-time studio photography business. However, deep down, I knew that wasn't my path or destiny either, and if I did it, I'd soon lose interest in another monotony of routine that didn't challenge my intellect. It didn't help that my landlord tried to evict me after he mistook the drying photographs in my darkroom for illicit pictures.

Somewhere deep inside, the memory of my childhood dream of doing something meaningful was still calling to be realized. There was a destiny out there waiting for me to find it. I was stuck and lost, but after some soul-searching, I decided I needed a profession that would allow for both creativity and intellectual stimulation. Something to engage both sides of my brain, so to speak. This realization made me smile. Maybe I was on to something.

TIME FOR CHANGE

My destiny still elusive, it was my generational turn to ponder the classic existential questions:

"Who am I?"

"Is there more to me than what I know and see?"

And the most crucial: "What is my purpose?" or better yet, "Is there even a purpose to be had?"

The intuitive sense of inner knowing pushed me forward to seek a greater understanding of myself, and over time, these thoughts took on a more serious tone and urgency. There was so much more to be known and understood, and I was aching and hungry for answers. I could have easily slid down the path of least resistance and embraced my Wall Street career; although many chose it, I felt it wasn't for me. Deep in my gut, I had yet to realize my potential, and I knew there was much more to unveil and learn. I was on a mission to discover who I was, and to uncover my purpose and meaning.

As far back as I remember, I've always been driven to seek self-knowledge. I ached to understand my finite existence in the context of a bigger picture. The process of self-discovery—continuously examining oneself through unfiltered lenses, and building awareness of blind spots and shortcomings—is arguably the most challenging strategy for self-betterment, but I needed to know who I was at my core and to find my purpose.

Early on in my twenties, I pored over everything from classics to inspirational literature, looking for answers. I read authors as disparate as the Dalai Lama and Viktor Frankl, Hermann Hesse, and Yogananda. This was an unanticipated effort on the part of an otherwise fun-loving and unscholarly young man. Still, what my destination was, or what it looked like, remained nebulous. I read the entirety of Hesse, and reread *Steppenwolf* and *Narcissus and Goldmund* many times, contemplating the duality of human nature. The enlightened (both book and protagonist) Siddhartha was so very satisfying to acquaint myself with. I related to something in all these books and their characters, which, in turn, made me wonder about my duality, and my own mystical nature. The idea of untapped inner potential—almost like a superhero before the great reveal—was enticing, and I sensed there was so much more to uncover than my present existence.

Man's Search for Meaning, written by Viktor Frankl—a Holocaust camp survivor who survived not only unbroken, but fortified by the experience—spoke to me directly and touched me on a visceral level. Frankl highlighted the primary importance of seeking meaning—even in the impossible conditions of Nazi concentration camps. His book has been one of the most influential of its kind, selling over twenty-four million copies and being translated into twenty-plus languages.

Frankl argued that despite suffering, we can always freely choose our attitude of how to cope and respond in any given situation and find meaning in any circumstance. He illuminates how we give our life meaning by choosing how we respond to adversity—the only free choice we might have left. His central theory is that a person's primary drive is not pursuit of pleasure or power, but rather a quest for meaning. Frankl identified three possible sources for this: work, love, and courage. He was fond of Friedrich Nietzsche's saying, "He who has a Why to live for can bear almost any How."

Frankl's writing fueled my own search for that elusive destiny that would give me meaning. If he could do it under the most difficult of circumstances, so could I. In these moments of contemplation, I remembered my childhood dream of wanting to accomplish something meaningful, be helpful, and make a positive impact in the world.

Together, Hesse's and Frankl's words became my primary driving force, preoccupying my fleeting time. Some deeper sense of inner knowing and elusive mystical energy was propelling me forward. I felt this with all my senses, and in my bones.

Many descriptive accounts have been written of achieving inner awakening and feelings of universal unity or oneness—from The Upanishads, to Meister Eckhart, to Walt Whitman. I could relate to these on an intellectual level, but that was not enough. I sought the actual experience, not the literary description of it. Although captivating, my reading did not shift my inner self; it just made me discouraged. Something was amiss—something I could not name. The only indication was the gaping hole I felt within my soul.

Ultimately, what helped me most was the practice of meditation. Although I had read about it in books, I had never given it a thought. However, synchronicity intervened. I met Bob, who was doing some carpentry at my mother's house. A guy my age, with similar interests in art and jazz, he lived in the neighborhood. We became fast friends, discussing philosophical doctrines, and soon our conversations turned to the concept of spirituality. Little did I know, Bob was an advanced spiritual seeker himself.

When he asked, seemingly nonchalantly, what I thought of the Buddhist concepts of reincarnation and karma, I dismissed him. Even though I had read about past lives and such, in reality it seemed too farfetched. I even began to question Bob's sensibilities. However, I grew intrigued when he spoke about his regular meditation practice and asked if I'd ever tried. That got my attention, and I asked for guidance. Bob suggested we sit together, and he offered to help with the basics. It seemed innocuous enough, so I went along.

With simple instructions, Bob suggested I sit in a comfortable chair with my eyes closed, and simply breathe for a few minutes. When my mind became distracted by stray thoughts, he recommended I consciously shift my focus to my incoming and outgoing breath. Doing this helped me regain a sense of calm, if only for a moment. He then suggested I try focusing my eyes on the flame of a candle to quiet my mind further. Whenever distracting thoughts popped up, I would open my eyes and fix my gaze on the flame. Strangely, that helped.

I later learned that concentrating on the flame stimulates the space between the eyes—the so-called Third Eye or *Ajna* in Sanskrit—which is said to be a direct link to higher consciousness and spiritual insight. I noticed warmth and a gentle sparkling movement in that area—startling at first but ultimately calming. This sensation led me to a deeper and more focused practice.

Strangely enough, sitting quietly and meditating felt familiar, as if this were not the first time, or even the first lifetime, I had done it. Maybe there was something to the past-life memories and reincarnation Bob talked about...who knew? And so, I began to practice on my own, more or less regularly. With time, my meditations became prolonged and profound. I was able to sit for extended periods without frequent interruptions from my "monkey mind." Vast Universe filled the quieted space. In the dark, at night, I would light a single candle and sit in a comfortable chair to experience the emptiness. I felt alone and maybe lonely at times, but also strangely happy and at peace. It was a welcome feeling. Afterward, it felt like stirring from a relaxing nap—without having been asleep. I was refreshed both physically and mentally. I embraced the practice of meditation.

My anxiety over finding answers to the pervasive angst and discontent gradually dissipated. At the same time, my Wall Street job grew ever less meaningful. I didn't care about it. Something was changing within me, and I wanted to know if there was more to this meditation practice—what was next?

FIRST MEDITATION CLASS

As my friendship with Bob progressed, we hung out more often, frequenting local jazz clubs, drinking beer, and discussing life—as one does. We even went on a few double-dates with our respective girlfriends. Bob was a painter as well as a carpenter, and we managed to set up a joint exhibit of his paintings and my photographs in a gallery in the West Village. I even sold one of my photographs to an art collector! The bizarre thing was that the collector did not choose any of what I considered to be my best pieces; instead, he honed in on a photograph I thought was quite average—and carried it reverentially away.-

In our discussions, Bob had mentioned a spiritual teaching he was studying—Agni yoga—and that a meditation and discussion class was held twice a week somewhere in Manhattan. I didn't know anything about Agni yoga, but Bob had guided me in a good direction up to this point and the class sounded like an interesting proposition.

Agni is the Hindu word for "god of fire," and Agni yoga is known as the yoga of fiery energy—the union of the individual with universal consciousness through responsible, directed thought. It teaches that the evolution of planetary consciousness is an urgent necessity and that, through individual striving, this evolution is possible for all humanity.

Agni yoga, which became known as "The Teaching of the Living Ethics" or "The Teaching of Life or Light," was initiated by Helena and Nicholas Roerich in 1920. That same year, they founded the Agni Yoga Society in New York, which became the channel for publishing their Living Ethics series. Rather than emphasizing physical practices, the Roerichs focused on applying fiery, conscious energy to everyday life as a path to both personal and planetary evolution. They framed spiritual growth within a grand cosmic context, weaving together ideas from science, Eastern religions, theosophy, and Russian cosmism. Their teachings were set forth in a series of books—abstract and metaphorical, filled with beautifully veiled prose that makes the wisdom challenging to extract. In other words, definitely not for me.

However, with some apprehension, I accepted the invitation to an Agni yoga meeting in a private apartment on the Upper East Side. The first meeting was set for seven sharp; I was anxiously early, and hungry. There was time to kill. I found a local pizza joint and inhaled two slices and a soda. There was still time, so I ordered a cannoli and finished half-read stories from the morning paper—but there was nothing there to hold my attention. My thoughts turned to the meeting and I felt a bit jittery, not knowing what to expect. Finally, it was time.

I knocked on the door and a pleasant middle-aged woman welcomed me. There were about ten people—milling around, talking, some sitting on the sofa in the living room near a baby grand piano, which I took as a welcome sign of old-world culture. A few awkward moments standing by myself passed thankfully quickly, as Bob noticed me and introduced me to the other attendees. Everyone was kind and welcoming. One person who came over was Nanette Hucknall. As we chatted, she seemed curious about my background and interests. Her interest seemed sincere, and she listened intently. I could feel her warmth somewhere in my soul—a new feeling. I liked and basked in it.

As the class began, I found a place to sit. The participants offered a short dedication to their teacher, Ralph Houston, who had been a student of the Roerichs and passed away from cancer several years before.

Although I had read about it, the idea of actually having a spiritual teacher was novel, and intriguing—I didn't know what to make of it, but was not repelled by any means. The group settled in to start meditation and I welcomed the quiet. Following a somewhat lengthy silence, the students reviewed readings from different Agni yoga books, and a lively discussion of the materials ensued. It seemed everyone had a different interpretation of the text, and I grew evermore confused.

Nanette's interpretations, however, stood out: they seemed somehow more grounded and pragmatic, and this resonated with my intellectual mindset. Regarding a sentence read from the Roerichs' book *Infinity*, "People are afraid most of all of expansion of consciousness...," Nanette expounded that much of humanity fears the vast unknown, and in this context, she equated consciousness with self-awareness at the center of our being. She went on to explain that we are only tiny specks with a finite existence in this infinite Cosmos, and merely attempting to comprehend this made most people uncomfortable: the very notion went against the intuitive self-centric universe we've created in our minds.

It was a great deal to take in, and I grew tired as the class ended the same way it began, with a closing silence; thankfully, this one was brief.

On the way out, I caught up with Nanette and—intellectually emboldened by all I'd learned—asked her how my finite individuality fit into the vast expanse of the Universe. She looked at me quizzically at first, then explained that it is our individual responsibility to expand our self-awareness and cultivate positive thinking—which, in turn, propels the collective evolution forward. The fascinating thing was, I not only heard her words but felt the warmth of her message.

She thanked me for the question, making me feel good and smart, and walked away. Somehow, her explanation and her way of thinking resonated with my intuitive understanding, and now there was a challenge to ponder—*our individual responsibility for propelling evolution forward.* I had received a brief, intuitive glimpse of my illusive path.

Walking home, I had time to think more carefully, to analyze the experience, and to compare it to what I'd read in books. Initially I hadn't been sure what to expect, but—somewhat to my surprise—nothing had felt alien or off. Instead, the group of people, the feeling of warmth, and the class itself were strangely familiar, and I felt comfortable in this new environment—although not as much with the readings from the books. As the class had progressed, the embodiment of unity, of being "at home," had come over me, and I welcomed the unanticipated sensation. It was a sense of profound belonging, of being one with the group...and beyond. I wanted more.

The original Sanskrit meaning of yoga is "unity" or oneness of all beings. It is this union of individual consciousness with universal consciousness that the adepts seek. Maybe that was the nature of my welcome-yet-unexpected experience—something I had only read about in books, but of which I had now received a taste. I continued attending classes, and over time, group meditation became second nature to me and I looked forward to these meetings.

Practicing meditation in a group was more focused, and certainly more profound. After several classes, I noticed a subtle sensation of warmth in my body best described as a gentle breeze—yet more like warm, sparkling energy tingling and flowing through me, simultaneously calming and invigorating. Talking with Nanette after class, she validated my experience, saying that indeed sometimes she had similar sensations moving through her physical body. She went on to say that sometimes she felt these just outside but close to her body, so much so that she recognized it with her inner senses. She explained that this was physical energy moving around and seemed surprised but pleased that I had been able to experience it.

HEARING THINGS

I continued attending Agni yoga classes, and in one class sensed tiny sparkles of light tingling throughout my being. It was as if electrons inside my nerve endings were dancing and emitting light. Then I heard a silent voice speak, asking me, "Why are you here?"

Without thinking, a spontaneous answer burst from within, "Because I want to know."

The voice replied, "You can do it," and then, in a blink, it was gone.

*Wow...*really? In that moment, even more so, I knew I was on the right path and going deeper within. I was genuinely happy for the first time in a long time.

I had not perceived this conversation with my physical senses—no one was speaking to me—but rather with my inner senses of hearing and seeing. Although everything seemed to return to normal when I opened my eyes, I knew something unusual had happened. I was unsure what it was, but for some reason, it wasn't shocking; instead, it was pleasing and comforting. In a strange way, it was like one of those déjà vu phenomena we all recognize at times. Somehow, this one left me with even more confidence that I was on the right path to new discoveries laying inside and ahead of me.

Of course, it's crucial to distinguish between fantasy and reality because our desires can be so powerful that they convince us to follow our lower nature—the part of ourselves driven by ego, imperfections, and base cravings—which ultimately hinder spiritual progress. Other people in class shared similar perceptions of seeing and hearing with their inner senses, and theirs sounded uncannily similar to mine. I also checked all sorts of literature and found that the Italian psychiatrist—and Dante's compatriot—Roberto Assagioli, described this type of sensation: *energies descend into images, and images descend into words.*[i] This description exactly mirrored my experience of inner hearing, reassuring me of its validity.

I was beginning to recognize the wisdom and the unexplored potential that was emerging within my conscious mind, the so-called *inner knowing*. As I grew more confident, developing a new sense of purpose and drive toward self-awareness, I realized the duality of my nature: the lower tendencies that constantly drag us away from the path to knowing ourselves, the higher tendencies that pull us forward and upward. This dualism mirrors the inner and outer realities of life, existing in parallel in all of us. Two sides of the same coin. How much more was there to discover and learn?

---

i Personal communication obtained by the author from Richard Schaub. The quote derives from Assagioli's personal notes, accessed by Richard Schaub in Assagioli's historically preserved archive in Florence.

HIGHER SELF LESSONS

The idea of the higher self is not limited to yoga or Eastern philosophies; it exists in nearly all belief systems. In Hinduism, it is called the Atman, the true self that is part of universal consciousness. Similarly, in Buddhism, it is seen as universal nondual consciousness. In more recent Western history, Dante described the Pilgrim's union with his higher self—his Beatrice—as a vision of "[t]he Love that moves the sun and the other stars."

Nanette became one of my closest friends, as she was genuinely interested in my thinking, questions, and wellbeing. She shared her spiritual insights, and I continued to have regular discussions with her. After several conversations, she gave me a copy of her writings, titled *Higher Self Lessons*. The very first lesson was called "Use of the Heart," which brought forward an abstract concept that made me curious. *How does one use the heart?* Did Nanette mean like a muscle, or something else? I asked and she explained that—like the mind and the intellect, which we know how to use and use every day—the heart is another energy center to be utilized in daily life, especially when interacting with others.

Mario: But how?

Nanette: Think of it like the warm energy you felt in class when we first met. Focus on the heart. Visualize shifting the energy downward, from your head, from your intellectual mind, into your heart. Then use it as a magnet when you work with people. When you feel that energy, project it outward to the person you are engaging with.

Mario: That's weird. What does it mean to project outward, to work like a magnet with people?

Nanette: It means to be more understanding of and interested in what someone is saying. The other person will sense it, just like you felt it when we first met. This is fiery energy that connects us on multiple levels, including the most physical one.

And with that, our conversation ended. I had no idea how she knew that I felt her warmth during our first meeting. I guess it was her heart that had radiated warmth. *Impressive!* I thought I'd give it a try, and after a few attempts, I began to feel warmth in the center of my chest. In engaging with others and projecting that warmth outward, there was now increased clarity and focus in my conversations, and with that came a newfound positivity. Fiery energy...really? *Astonishing.*

NEW BEGINNINGS

After I had attended a few more Agni yoga meetings, the group drifted apart as some people went their separate ways. Nanette was on sabbatical in Europe at that time. One evening, a close friend from class, Peter, approached me and suggested starting a new class based on Nanette's lessons and writings on the higher self. I was totally on board with it and agreed to join. As a novice and a new member to the group, I was somewhat surprised and honored that I was asked to join this venture.

We held our first meeting with a few other interested members at Peter's home in the suburbs of Long Island, an unfamiliar territory to me. He had a nice house with a glorious backyard swimming pool, and we all went for a dip, as it was a warm spring day. It was refreshing, and later we bonded over brunch, lounging in the sun without the distracting noises of the city. Peter was a decent guy and over the years we became close, and we keep in touch to this day. Unfortunately, Bob was not interested in joining our new group, and our friendship eventually faded away.

During this meeting, the group established rules for holding our classes, which included taking turns leading, providing honest feedback, and being respectful of each other's spiritual insights. The protocol we devised was that we would meditate together on a concept or experience one of us had, usually stemming from one of the written lessons. We would then share with the group. In turn, there would be a short five-minute silent reflection, and everyone would—without judgment—offer their insight. Usually there were different interpretations, but more often than not, singular wisdom emerged that resonated with the situation at hand. Now, many years later, the structure in my classes remains essentially the same, with the exception that I lead and answer most of the questions from my students.

Unable to travel to Long Island regularly, we decided to hold meetings at Ingmar's, who graciously offered his apartment in the city. Ingmar was a single guy from Norway and had a comfortable place with lots of natural light. Class structure established, we also decided it would be held at the same time as the Agni yoga sessions, from seven to eight thirty in the evening.

In one of the first classes, we discussed how we visualize our higher self. An image I held was that my higher self was not yet a fully realized part of my being, my consciousness—yet it was in me, it was who I was. Others envisioned their higher self as a wise being standing next to them. There was long discussion on this topic with differing points of view, but in the end, we concluded that diverse concepts are valid interpretations, as the essential point was to recognize and work with all these energies that are within us all.

On the corner near Ingmar's building, there was a very pleasant Greek diner a few of us frequented after class for late supper and casual conversations that furthered our friendships. This small group of dedicated individuals eventually grew to become the core of the Higher Self Yoga community we have today.

After Nanette returned from Europe, she was initially stumped (and possibly even miffed!) that we had made such of big deal out of her writings, and had even started a new class without telling her. Still, there was a noticeable twinkle in her eye, suggesting she was happy. She eventually took over leading the class—it was, after all, on the lessons she had written—and the meetings moved to her apartment. What was fascinating about Nanette's way of teaching was that she not only explained theory in a way that seemed rational and easy to understand, but she also provided practical step-by-step guidance on how to incorporate theory into daily practice. These lessons eventually became the core of the Higher Self Yoga teaching Nanette founded, and which I have followed since the beginning, now for over forty years.

I continued to attend her classes with the original group. More new students came in, having heard about the class by word of mouth. This was an exhilarating period where we learned about the existence of our higher selves—the wisdom each of us holds within, and its many practical applications in our daily lives, as was the case in point with the use of the heart energy I had experimented with. Together, we explored inner wisdom of the heart and the mind, at the core of the higher self. With our hearts we feel warmth and beauty, and with our minds we comprehend that experience. Merging of the heart and the mind energies is the ultimate synthesis of the two core aspects of the higher self. I continued to discover the innermost essence of my being, and awaken the vast knowledge and power it held.

When Nanette left the city and moved to the Berkshires, where she now lives and continues to teach, I stayed in touch. The New York City class continued with many students now gathering in my apartment every Thursday evening. I had become responsible for teaching and leading.

It says in the *Tao Te Ching*, "When the student is ready, the teacher will appear," but the opposite is also true: when the teacher is ready, the students come. During this period, and to my surprise, more students arrived seeking guidance in the practice of meditation and the process of uncovering their inner wisdom. Most learned about the classes by word of mouth, from other students and friends, old and new.

MY WAY

Like Dante's protagonist, the Pilgrim—who emerged from the dark woods and glimpsed the luminosity of the stars ahead of him—I was also moving out of my despair, my own version of Hell. Hopeful, I saw light at the end of what felt like a long, dark tunnel: the prospect of a new beginning with all its (still quite vague and unformed) promises stretching ahead of me.

Searching for definition, one day I asked Nanette, "What is the meaning of the higher self you speak about in your lessons, and how does it apply to me?"

She explained: "The higher self is your inner core of wisdom. It's your wise being, if you wish. It is all the positive accumulations—the knowledge and the wisdom we carry, unbeknownst to us. If you are able to consciously access the wisdom of your higher self, you will be able to accomplish anything you put your mind to." She went on, somewhat mysteriously, "Read Dante's *Divine Comedy*, and you will understand the path you must travel."

And with that, she left me wondering and wanting to know more.

I began rereading Dante with new eyes, so to speak. His *Divine Comedy* is an epic poem that follows the protagonist, the Pilgrim—a personification of the spiritual seeker—on his arduous mountain climb. This pilgrimage illustrates one's ultimate union with the higher self, beautifully depicted in the final *Paradiso* section of the poem.

As I delved into the text, I saw how Dante's portrayal provided not just a beautiful, but a practical, roadmap for connecting with one's inner wisdom and energies—and that my own search for meaning was intricately linked to the search for my higher self, my innate wisdom. Late one night, reading the *Paradiso*, I had a visceral sensation of physically merging with the Pilgrim. There were sparks of light surrounding our figures melding into one, and this tingling energy made me feel hopeful. I identified with the Pilgrim, the seeker, and his search for higher wisdom—his higher self. I was formulating my own path forward—I was *seeking*.

THE MOUNTAIN

My personal goal, like the Pilgrim's, was to find and live in union with my higher wisdom—my heart and my mind in synthesis as expression of my higher self. The Pilgrim's mountain climb to the summit illuminates his final and ultimate union with his higher self, his inner Beatrice. At that moment, the Pilgrim merges, becoming one with the mystical energies of the Universe. But not so fast: before ascending to the summit, there is the obligatory passage through Hell, followed by the transformative stages of Purgatory. I had a long way to go, but now I had a roadmap to follow, and I was inspired.

On his journey to understanding, the Pilgrim is helped by two guides: Virgil, who represents human reason and leads him through Hell and Purgatory (the human experience); Beatrice, who represents his higher self, taking over from Virgil and guiding the Pilgrim through the final stages of the ascent to the summit of the mountain.

In the realm of Hell, the Pilgrim must observe and recognize the many lower human characteristics. It is only when he realizes that human actions have consequences, and that we all have lower-nature tendencies, that he is allowed to move to the next stage of the mountain climb, Purgatory.

We define lower-nature characteristics as patterns and behaviors that negatively impact our lives. Greed, anger, and violence drain our energy, distract, and divert us from our innate purpose. They are personality tendencies that manifest as thoughts, judgments, and actions pulling us away from our spiritual center and from our striving, our ascent. Negative traits give us a false sense of separation from others and incite selfish behavior. Though we all have them, they differ from individual to individual. Each of us needs to recognize our own lower nature for our unique process of transformation to begin.

Wading through Purgatory begins this process of individual transformation, wherein we identify specific elements of our lower nature and, instead of indulging them, willfully choose the opposite—positive—behaviors. When we do, we refine our lower nature by transforming negative aspects into positive ones. In medieval times, this was likened to the alchemical process of transmuting lead into gold.

Toward the end of *Purgatory*, the Pilgrim reaches a point where Virgil is no longer capable of guiding him. Although reason and intellect can be immensely helpful in the process of overcoming our negative qualities, and are indispensable during the wade through Purgatory, they have limitations and are insufficient in guiding the seeker through the very last stage of extricating themself from the mundane, and stepping into the light of Beatrice. The seeker must then rely more on their heart to connect with the mystical powers of the climb. Therefore, Virgil moves aside, and Beatrice—the embodiment of light—takes over. She represents the Pilgrim's higher self and is his inner guide up the mountain toward the summit.

THE SUMMIT

Climbing the steep mountain out of Purgatory, the Pilgrim develops a connection to his heart. This enables him to connect to Beatrice—who is not external, like Virgil, but represents a connection to the numinous within Dante himself. From this point forward, the Pilgrim is in fact alone—human reason (in the form of Virgil) has left him—and singlehandedly must climb to the summit to reach ultimate union with his higher self. As he travels, the Pilgrim maintains an inner dialogue with Beatrice, who guides him on his journey by describing the obstacles ahead.

Transforming his negative patterns and fears as he ascends the mountain, climbing becomes ever easier. He feels physically lighter and freer. However, the hard labor of self-transformation continues as he approaches the summit, as his ego persistently influences him, tying him to the limitations of his physical self. Thankfully, Beatrice comes to his aid, advising him to stop thinking and attempting to rationally analyze—and instead to simply give himself up to feeling and experiencing the mystical energies that surround them. At this point in the journey, Beatrice offers the Pilgrim her hand and leads him to the summit (*Illustration 1*).

Illustration 1. Beatrice guiding Dante to Paradise.[ii]

---

ii 14th century Venetian miniature, Biblioteca Marciana, Venice: *Beatrice guida Dante*. Wikimedia Commons. Retrieved July 4, 2025, from https://commons.wikimedia.org/w/index.php?title=File:Beatrice_guida_Dante.jpg&oldid=1031131356.

It is a surrender of sorts. At this advanced stage of his journey, it is more important for the Pilgrim to trust his heightening spiritual senses, rather than hold on to familiar thinking patterns and rationalizations. Many seekers resist this subtle shift because it often feels like relinquishing control. However, it is most profound—trust your experiential truths!

It is when Pilgrim reaches the summit of the mountain that he finally becomes one with Beatrice, the embodiment of his higher self—he has now integrated his inner wisdom into his consciousness. This union opens him to energy levels that are entirely metaphysical, not descriptive—beyond words.

As the journey reaches its end, Pilgrim and Beatrice are in spiritual union, dancing in meditation, bathed in light. This union illuminates the Pilgrim's mind and heart with the truth, allowing him to not merely see, but to experience the ultimate vision of *Divine Love—the Love that moves the sun and the stars.*

It is imperative to remember that, unbeknownst to him, Pilgrim's higher self, Beatrice, is present with him throughout the entire journey. But it is only when, through striving upward, we awaken the connection to our higher self that it becomes an integral element of our being and walks with us each day. When faced with any obstacle, or when in doubt about making the right decision, all we must do is take a mental nanosecond to reconnect and our bring inner-wisdom mind to the forefront of awareness. Decisions become increasingly balanced and easier to make. The more we develop the connection with our higher self, the stronger it becomes, and the easier it is to make the right decision and to act in alignment with our higher principles.

At a certain point, with practice and time, the energies of the higher self—the heart and the mind—become integrated into the neuronal pathways of the physical brain and into our immediate awareness. As this occurs, we live in harmony with our inner wisdom. This is the result of neuroplasticity—a scientifically proven fact—the capacity of the brain to build new neuronal pathways and alter existing ones throughout one's life. The practice of meditation helps to establish and alter thinking patterns; it can break old habits and redirect them to new ways of processing information.

Dante's profound concept—of spiritual advancement represented as a laborious climb up a steep mountain—resonated for me in the drawing *The Human Mountain* by the early-twentieth-century Swedish artist Edward Munch (who became pop-culture famous with another drawing of his, *The Scream*). *The Human Mountain* (*Illustration 2*), shows a multitude of people at various stages of their climb toward the light at the summit. At the foot of the mountain is a tangled mass of bodies suffering in the hell of mundane existence—some in motion, others slumped in despair. Farther up are those striving to free themselves, reaching heavenward. At the top of the mountain we find the seeker, bathed in light with arms outstretched toward the sun and the light of the Universe.

Illustration 2. The Human Mountain by Edward Munch[iii]

iii *The Human Mountain*, Edvard Munch, 1909-1910, Aquarelle on paper, Munchmuseet Cat. No. MM.T.02549.

Part 2

THE JOURNEY

When you are ready to begin to scale the
mountainside, do not come back
this way; the rising sun will show you where to climb.

DANTE (*PURGATORY*, CANTO I, 107-108)

DISCOVERING MY PURPOSE

Just like the Pilgrim, I was working my way up the mountain, slowly, but always ascending. Having identified my spiritual practice and a path forward, I now needed to find my ever-elusive destiny that would move me away from the hell of Wall Street toward my life's purpose.

At this point, I was making a real effort to carve out time for my practice of meditating several times a day. Before leaving for work at the bank in the morning, I'd try to sit for a short meditation to start off the day. During lunch hour, I would often sneak into Trinity Church on the corner of Broadway and Wall Street for half an hour of contemplation. The evenings, however, offered the longest and most fruitful time to practice. At the end of the day, as life outside quieted down, I was physically and mentally tired. My monkey mind offered the least resistance, and it was easier to focus and turn attention toward my inner wisdom, hoping for inspiration. This was when I had my best insights.

Late one night, while quietly siting in my favorite chair, I experienced a brief but nagging vision of myself looking at some books. *Strange*. The vision didn't make much sense, so I dismissed it. But several days later, during my lunch break—while mindlessly browsing the magazine section in a bookstore on Broadway—I came across a color layout of medical photographs of the human brain shown in health and in illness. Immediately, I felt that by-now-familiar tingling in my nerve endings. Wow! *Again.* The title of the article was "Breakthrough in Science." Inexplicable excitement overcame me as I leafed through the pages. I couldn't stop looking at the images of the brain, so detailed and so colorful! It was my first encounter with the merging of photography and medicine, of art and science, the two seeming opposites working in union to help identify and cure heretofore untreatable illnesses.

It was an intense and immediate recognition of synchronicity at play. And more important, a realization of my new calling! In that instant, I knew my love and understanding of photography, coupled with the field of medical sciences, seamlessly combined creativity and intellect in one career—which was precisely what I had been unconsciously searching for! This realization shook me so hard that I almost forgot to pay for the magazine.

Inspired and curious, I began researching different imaging techniques used in medicine and in scientific study. I discovered several career options, including becoming an X-ray technician, a scientist, or a medical doctor. Becoming a technician seemed too pedestrian. Medical school, on the other hand, although appealing, felt too daunting. That left me enthusiastic about the middle way, and I was drawn to experimental medical sciences as my path forward. If the Pilgrim could do it, so could I. After all, Dante taught that Pilgrim's journey is possible for everyman. Paying attention to synchronicity, combined with my drive, striving, and self-awareness were paying off.

There was an uncanny familiarity and recognition in pursuing the medical sciences, as if I'd been there before. In a way, I was predisposed to study science; it was in my DNA. Growing up, I saw the many medical books and actual human bones displayed in the *vitrine* at my grandparents' home—all my uncles and aunts had studied medicine and become physicians. My father was a chemical engineer and my mother, an economist. It was in my genes to undertake this challenge. I also thought that understanding and studying the human body would reveal its secret inner metaphysical workings—something akin to the discovery of the philosopher's stone, a magical medicinal potion, similar to the way alchemists believed in transmuting lead into gold. I wanted to understand my human self at its core, and in the context of finite time. And so, with all my heart, I decided to become a scientist.

One kind of men see nothing but the infinite and ignore themselves.
The other see only themselves and ignore the infinite.
Those who rightly see both compose the true wise man.

—Blaise Pascal, *Pensées, Brunschvicg #267*,
translated by W. F. Trotter

There was a deeper purpose in choosing science as a career. It would fulfill my lifelong desire to make a positive contribution and be of service. However, to become a scientist, I had to start at the beginning. First, I had to return to school and learn new skills, and it would take at least four years to earn even a bachelor's degree in biology. I reflected on the options, researched different possibilities, and mulled over my decision. I was certain this was the right path for me, and it would lead to a fulfilling career, one of meaningful purpose. But how to make it happen?

Mirroring the Pilgrim's climb, I tapped into wisdom I didn't know I possessed; my inner self knew me better than I did. That moment of insight—when I connected with my wisdom in meditation and saw myself browsing through books—completely changed my life's trajectory. This was a big moment of synchronicity, and the more I practiced meditation, the more I became open to recognizing and following signs like this in my everyday life. From that point onward, I had a sense that my life was being guided in the right direction, by some invisible force. New doors opened. I started seeing my life's purpose unfolding before me. I was content, even happy, but knew it was only the beginning of many challenges and adventures—climbing the mountain and following the Pilgrim's path.

BACK TO SCHOOL

I continued my journey, faced with the difficult climb up my own steep mountain, but still working toward my goal of metaphysical unity.

With an unclouded vision of a career in science, I would pursue a degree in biology with a chemistry minor—essentially a pre-med curriculum with a heavy emphasis on sciences, including advanced courses in physics and math. My search for the right school led me to Hunter College, which offered a broad range of science courses in the evenings that allowed me to test the waters and continue working for the time being. Hunter, being part of the City University of New York (CUNY) system, was more affordable than most. Additionally, the college had an excellent reputation for pre-med studies, so I enrolled in several introductory science courses.

The student body was the proverbial melting pot of diverse cultures and languages, just like New York City itself, and I was totally at home, despite being older than the average student. It was a collegial place, a completely different environment from the Wall Street foreign exchange trading floor and its hustle of winning and losing, the zero-sum game. I rushed out of work to be on time for evening lectures, eating a snack on the go to avoid being distracted by an empty stomach during class.

Staying focused and comprehending information I'd never encountered before took effort, which made me nervous and doubtful about my academic prowess. I was still working at the bank, my Wall Street coworkers seemed increasingly distant and irrelevant, and I was always exhausted. It would be a steep climb, and it felt just like the Pilgrim's laborious progress out of Hell. The comparison gave me motivation to keep going.

As I ascended my mountain of redemption, I kept questioning myself. *Would I be able to make it?* Every time my fears crept up, I remembered that first instance of synchronicity—that moment in the bookstore—and the recognition that I was pursuing the right course of action gave me strength to continue without doubting myself too badly. Like the Pilgrim on his mountain climb, I realized that once started, there was no turning back, only moving forward toward an exciting, albeit uncertain future.

As I committed to the new path, fragments of memories assembled in my mind. Walking the hallways of Hunter, I had an odd recollection, beyond mere familiarity or *déjà vu*. It was a stronger sensation of having walked these same hallways before, without being able to recall when or where. These odd, discombobulating visions persisted for several weeks and even popped up in my dreams.

One day, during an exam, as I paused for a moment of reflection and looked out the window down Lexington Avenue, a peculiar memory of an early childhood dream flashed across my mind. I remembered this exact moment of seeing myself taking this very same exam, sitting in this chair, and looking out the window! *Wow...* So strange and inexplicable, momentarily stirring me up, this vision sparked an instant recognition that I was in the right place, at the right moment in my life's journey, fulfilling my destiny.

The realization made me smile. I continued with the exam, joyful and at peace. This memory, and other moments of synchronicity, remain embedded in my mind, always reminding me that I was following my destiny and purpose.

Having never been exposed to any science classes, I enrolled in the Principles of Biology, a comprehensive, two-semester course on the biological processes that support human life. It was loads of completely new knowledge, but I loved it, as I was discovering what makes me, the human being, tick at a basic physical level. Magically captivating, and now I was hooked! The thick textbook had detailed illustrations of complex principles, including images that reminded me once again of the moment of synchronicity in the bookstore that changed my life's trajectory.

After successfully completing a year of evening courses, I grew more confident about quitting my day job and continuing to study at Hunter full-time. It was a decision made with immense pleasure, as leaving Wall Street felt like shedding a heavy burden. Though hardships lay ahead, I was determined to face them. I was not working anymore, I was a student, studying, feeling free, and moving ever closer to my destiny. This was happiness!

My continued coursework at Hunter was not only challenging but extremely competitive. I struggled, as there was much to learn. Most of my classmates were pre-med students—younger, bright, and all competing for high grades that would help them gain admission to a prestigious medical school. Consequently, the average exam scores were high, and tough to achieve. Despite the pressure, I appreciated the scholarly atmosphere, discovered my own competitive spirit, and studied much harder. I was ambitious to succeed and make my dream come true.

One of the toughest classes was organic chemistry: a watershed for many students who would struggle to pass and drop out. I too was struggling, but fortunate to hook up with a study group that met regularly in the library. We worked together to comprehend the complex concepts, and while we were all in competition for good grades, there was a sense of camaraderie and support. It was in this environment that my intellect thrived, and I look back fondly on these moments. The pleasure of collaborating stays with me to this day.

I continued my meditation practice most evenings before bed, sitting in front of my modest shrine—not much more than a small statue of the Buddha and few pictures, illuminated by a couple of tea candles and the ambient city lights. I often found inner peace in these moments of solitude, peace with myself and the world that forged a deep connection to my inner wisdom and my higher self.

Sometimes my meditation practice was more specific, as I would focus on a question or problem I struggled to understand—a method in Buddhism called Vipassana or clear-seeing. In these moments, I would intentionally bring the question I struggled with to the elevated mental plane of the higher self, which helped connect to a vaster knowledge and intuitive understanding. In these instances, I could easily comprehend and synthesize new concepts, the meaning of which I couldn't grasp from reading textbooks or attending lectures. It felt like solving a puzzle where the different pieces fit into their respective places in my mind's eye, allowing a complete picture to emerge.

For instance, when I was struggling to solve a chemistry problem, I might see and understand how different molecules came together in a specific reaction to form the intended end product. Similarly, I could conceptualize the necessary steps for creating a physiological outcome in a biological scenario. Often, the ideas and concepts I was having difficulty comprehending would surface in my dreams. I would wake up knowing and able to visualize the solution to a problem I had been struggling with, like how a specific chemical reaction produces the intended product.

THE AHA! MOMENT

During one lecture on the human immunodeficiency virus (HIV), given by a professor I greatly admired for his passion and clarity of presentation, I heard a slight buzz in my ears as the sounds in the lecture hall faded away. It was like a bolt of energy pulsating through my body. It lasted only an instant—although it felt longer—and flooded me with new awareness, as if someone had commanded me to "Pay attention!" I recognized the sensation from my early Agni yoga classes, when inner wisdom descended and pointed the way to me.

I straightened up and listened with renewed interest. What was the professor talking about that was so important at this exact moment? He was, in fact, explaining the life cycle of HIV and how the virus systematically invades and destroys the immune system of the infected person, ultimately leading to death. Normally, the immune system functions as our protection against foreign invaders, such as bacteria and viruses, but HIV was insidious: it was hijacking the very immune cells that were supposed to combat it and using them to replicate itself.

There was no treatment, only urgent scientific research into drugs that could slow down the infection and its devastating consequences. The goal, of course, was to find a vaccine to prevent the infection altogether—but the research was just beginning to ramp up. This was the late 1980s, a devastating period of the AIDS pandemic that destroyed many lives, especially in the gay community, which was most vulnerable. Many people suffered from this horrible illness—which took the lives of some of the most creative individuals of a generation—including actors like Anthony Perkins and Rock Hudson, the lead singer of Queen, Freddie Mercury, and the world-renowned ballet dancer Rudolf Nureyev, among so many others. No-one was spared.

As the lecture continued, the professor offered detailed explanations and illustrations of how the virus infects various cell types in the body, eventually killing them all. It was these details of infection and the challenge of stopping it that I found fascinating. This was not a mere metaphor for how the virus turns our own immune protection against itself—it was real. I could envision the challenges posed by this. At that instant, I heard myself say, "That's it!" This was what I wanted to research and study, this would be my career in science.

It dawned on me again that it wasn't just an intellectually stimulating challenge I was looking for; I wanted to contribute to solving a problem that would alleviate the suffering caused by the ongoing pandemic. *This was my calling.* Deep inside my soul, I knew it was the right thing to do. This was what I wanted to do—no question! My wisdom, mind, and heart—working in unison—had alerted me to pay attention at the right moment. This realization marked another new but congruous beginning in my life, setting me on a path toward graduate school and biomedical research focused on curing HIV and AIDS.

During my second year at Hunter, to gain some much-desired, real-life, hands-on laboratory experience, I contacted the volunteer office at Cornell Medical School, which connected me with the laboratory studying the effects of tobacco use on human physiology. Following an interview with the head of the lab, I was accepted as a research assistant and began conducting research that had direct relevance to human health. After introductory theoretical background learning, I started hands-on laboratory testing of the effects of tobacco exposure on human cell biology and its immune system. *How cool is that!* I spent countless hours, evenings, and even some all-nighters, learning and conducting experiments at Cornell.

Doing actual wet-lab research with my own hands and seeing my own test results ticking out of the printer was a most extraordinary moment. It doesn't get more real or any better than that. For the first time ever, I was finding results no one else had seen before. This was a striking, fiery experience, and I wanted and needed to repeat that moment, many times over, forever—I was hooked on doing relevant biomedical research. As the art of science and the healing art of medicine merged seamlessly into biomedical research, I had my *eureka* moment!

Witnessing the head of the lab formulating novel hypotheses and conducting research to prove or disprove her theories was eye-opening education in its own right. In those moments, watching the work of scientific discovery unfold before my eyes, I recognized my ambition to have my own lab and conduct independent research, generating and testing my own ideas and hypotheses. My contribution at Cornell eventually led to a co-authored manuscript published in a prestigious peer-reviewed journal and a recommendation letter from the head of the lab, which eventually contributed to my graduate school application.

Walking through the hospital corridors at Cornell was a different kind of déjà vu than that of Hunter hallways. I felt at home, finally—destination reached! Surrounded by doctors, nurses, patients—and on top of that, wearing a white lab coat, not a suit and tie—gave me a sense of belonging, of importance, of finally meeting my destiny. It went a little (or maybe a lot) to my head. My ego was having fun, dancing circles around me: important work was being done and I got to be part of it! I was enjoying my ego-boosting. But deep down, I knew better—and just like the Pilgrim in Purgatory transforming lower ego impulses into positive attributes, I thought about all the people who were suffering and dying and soon realized there was nothing more important than my desire to be of service and contribute to the fight against AIDS.

Returning to Hunter snapped me back to reality as the courses became more challenging, especially with the added time I was spending in the lab at Cornell. On top of that, in need of income, I had to expand my commercial photography business. All this left me worn out, but I continued to meditate as often as possible, which helped restore my energy levels and cognition, and kept fatigue at bay. While some college courses were naturally more difficult than others, I found advanced physics and chemistry particularly trying. Hard work was never a problem—I was committed—but to succeed, I had to motivate myself to learn what I had previously considered irrelevant subjects. In a way, I enjoyed overcoming these obstacles because it allowed me to discover my strengths and weaknesses and uncover my true self.

As in the past, I continued to receive insights and images during contemplation time and in dreams. These were particularly helpful for identifying the way forward whenever I felt blocked. One image that crystalized in my inner sense of seeing was of two people sitting at a table with open books between them, each holding a notebook. I interpreted this to mean that if I wanted to succeed academically, I needed a partner.

I decided to hire graduate student tutors with expertise in the subjects I struggled with. This made conceptualizing problem-solving easy and enjoyable, as these guys could explain the nebulous concepts in a way that made sense. I looked forward to our sessions, where I grasped and understood knowledge previously elusive to me. I started to excel in challenging subjects like organic chemistry. My grades improved, my GPA was high, and my self-confidence remained intact. During the final year at Hunter, I completed several demanding advanced courses, graduating with a minor in chemistry and honors in biology.

It was time to find a postgraduate doctoral program that would allow me independent research, ideally one associated with a medical school. Having secured a couple of highly regarded recommendation letters, I began the application process. Graduate program application was an anxiety-inducing endeavor—I could only wait in helpless anticipation. It was a time of uncertainty as initial rejection letters arrived from the more prestigious universities. Although disappointed, I reassured myself that I had tried for the best.

Finally, interview invitations arrived, and after visiting several medical colleges, I was accepted into a few graduate programs. I decided to enroll in Rutgers Medical School in Newark, New Jersey, which was close to home, my weekly meditation classes, and my friends. Rutgers had a prestigious graduate program in biomedical research, and it was a good medical school that promised exposure to relevant study of human physiology. I enrolled in the fall, without any break to take stock or reflect.

Finally, I had climbed out of the morass of Wall Street—mirroring the Pilgrim's journey out of Hell—with glimpses of light and stars ahead of me.

HEART MIND SYNTHESIS

I wondered whether graduate school would be as rewarding and exciting as my experience at Hunter College or if it would be completely different. One major difference was that the program offered an annual stipend, which meant I no longer had to hustle for extra income—and I happily ended my commercial photography career. Now I could devote all my energy to studying and laboratory experiments that would lead to an academic degree allowing me to conduct independent research.

The first two years were comprised of relatively straightforward courses, and I participated in several introductory rotations through different laboratories. The theoretical knowledge was more focused and specific, emphasizing different experimental and technical methodologies. I found this particularly interesting, as I was learning how different research ideas were formulated and assessed. The mandatory laboratory rotations were designed to familiarize students with the array of departmental research interests and help choose a laboratory to match each student's interests.

The laboratories were led primarily by faculty members managing research for their funded projects. Each lab's size depended on the grant funding it had secured, typically obtained through the National Institutes of Health, the largest governmental sciences funding agency. The staff included technicians, postdoctoral fellows, and graduate students. After completing several rotations, I narrowed my options to two. However, I was having a challenging time deciding which one to choose. It was a major commitment—not only because I was to spend the next five-plus years there, but it would likely shape my future research career.

One laboratory was conducting research on the cellular immunology of HIV, which I found remarkably interesting and wanted to study; however, several personalities conflicted with my character, and office politics were not my forte. Conversely, the research projects in the second lab weren't of much interest to me, but the scientist in charge was someone I could easily get along with. It was a friendly and easy-going atmosphere into which I could comfortably fit. The two options felt completely different, and I was hard-pressed to select a laboratory and mentor for my doctoral thesis.

I was at a crossroads, and time was running out. I was facing a dilemma and needed help, but I alone could decide my future. I thought that by using my intellect and rational or mundane mind, the process of choosing would be easy and quick—so I made an extensive list of pros and cons for each lab. I went to the Violet Café in Washington Square Park and pondered the items on my list. The serene atmosphere of the surrounding park and the café, which had low-level background noise, provided a conducive environment for analysis and necessary breaks.

After one full day of trying to use my rational mind to evaluate the list, I realized I was being drawn in one direction—toward the second, seemingly more comfortable, lab environment. Still, something was amiss, but what? Why was I so concerned with my personal comfort that out of fear of facing potential unpleasantness, I would give up doing HIV research, which was my aspiration? It dawned on me that I was listening to my lower-ego nature, to my personal desires and fears, rather than to my higher nature. I recalled my conversations with Nanette—now a distant memory—and her lessons and practice for using my heart energy. Like the Pilgrim on his Mountain climb, it was time to summon my inner Beatrice to lead me.

The heart and the higher mind are the essential energies at the core of the higher self, which—often unbeknown to us—are available at all times. This concept is at the center of the Hindu devotional spiritual practice of Bhakti yoga, which teaches the use of the heart as the way to achieve union with one's higher self. On the other hand, the practice of Raja yoga teaches the use of the higher mind and the intellect as a gateway toward union with one's higher self. Both are ancient yogic traditions, tried and tested. In the Western world, they were first taught and published by Swami Vivekananda, but their origins are in the Bhagavad Gita and the Upanishads, foundational spiritual Hindu texts dating back thousands of years. They are the basis of the wisdom that teaches the everyday use of the heart and the mind, which, with practice, coalesces into heart-mind synthesis—a synergy at the center of accessing one's higher consciousness and achieving mystical union with one's higher self. To reach the summit of the Mountain, the Pilgrim needs both Virgil and Beatrice, higher mind and higher heart, in unison.

The subtle differences between our mundane mind and higher mind further complicate the process. The former tends to our daily needs and is influenced by our fears, hang-ups, history, and self-imposed limitations. The mundane mind can serve us only so far, giving the illusion of control, a false sense of achievement, and temporary happiness. The latter—our higher mind—is part of our higher self and is limitless.

In Agni yoga, the mundane mind connects to the higher mind via the Antahkarana bridge. Also known as a bridge of light or consciousness, it serves as a dynamic pathway from the personality of the lower self to the wisdom of the higher self, influencing positive thoughts and actions. This energetic connection is strengthened through spiritual development and practice.

Had I been a more advanced practitioner at the time, I would have realized the higher mind and the heart work in concert—not opposition—and that I'd been listening all along to my mundane mind or intellect, influenced by my fears and psychological hang-ups.

Though I thought I would never be able to choose, I persevered. And, after several days—on a subtle level—these seemingly opposing forces merged into a more unified experience, one of ease. It wasn't that I didn't care anymore, but something eased inside of me: I enjoyed walks in the park and watching people, without worry of impending doom. I was less stressed and more comfortable making a choice that now seemed within reach. I realized it wasn't a matter of life or death, and that in the end, whatever my decision, it would turn out for the best. I had begun to trust myself and to become more confident in my ability to make the right choice. I was traveling on the Antahkarana bridge, reaching my higher nature.

In the end, I took my pile of written notes, the pros and the cons for each lab, tore them up, and tossed them into the garbage. At that moment, a sense of freedom, relief, and peace came over me and it became clear that my interest in the research was more important than my personality preferences. I had been fascinated by HIV research ever since that *Aha!* moment during the lecture at Hunter, and I was determined to pursue it—decision made!

It felt as if my heart desire had won out. However, in reality, I was able to make the decision by merging the energies of my heart with my higher mind, working with each—separately at first, and eventually achieving equilibrium and synthesis between the two. My heart—my inner Beatrice—guided me through the clamor of mundane thoughts until I reached the blissful realm of the higher mind. This was an important experiential lesson demonstrating how each energy is different from the other and how it feels when the two are incongruent versus when they balance and coalesce.

Finally in the right lab, I joyfully immersed myself in the HIV work I was meant to do. My doctoral thesis project was aimed at evaluating the cellular conditions that would protect the human immune system from HIV infection, eventually eradicating the virus. I was happy and excited, as my work now involved considerable theoretical research followed by formulating, designing, and executing experiments. My time was spent thinking and using my rational mind to design and perform experiments and evaluate the results. Everything was going well and I was having a good time.

However, I gradually grew restless. Something was missing, and soon enough I remembered that using only my rational mind was not enough. There was a certain emptiness within my being, my very soul. My heart was unengaged, and I needed—and wanted—to activate that energy and bring it into balance with my mind, as I had done before. My mind was stimulated enough, but it was confined to an academic environment isolated from real people—whom my research ultimately aimed to help. I needed human contact and heart connection to gain balance.

Somewhat reluctantly, I decided to volunteer, in hopes of uniting my heart with my intellect and mind. I summoned up courage and walked down the corridor from the lab to the hospital's newborn isolation ward, where babies—separated from their mothers because of drug or alcohol abuse—were suffering painful withdrawal symptoms passed on to them *in utero*. I was nervous and apprehensive as I entered the ward, not knowing what to expect. The room was filled with cribs, and in each was a newborn, some crying out in pain. I stood, frozen, until a nurse saw me and came over, saying, "Don't be afraid—pick one up and hold it."

Seeing my hesitation, she picked a baby girl and put her in my arms. She told me I could sit down in a rocking chair and soothe the infant by tenderly touching her hand or cheek.

"Don't be afraid, they just need love," she said, and with that, left me alone, holding the little human.

As I looked at the newborn, there was an instant moment of heart connection and recognition, something I had never experienced before. That infant was suffering and needed to be comforted, reassured, and above all, to feel loved. With that recognition, tears came to my eyes—I had never experienced such intense emotion and happiness. Even as I write this—looking for the right words—once again, all the emotion of that moment returns. It was an instant heart-to-heart connection, the greatest feeling I've known. I came to experience firsthand Dante's "Divine love," a love that "Moves the Sun and the Stars."

I gently touched the baby's tiny face and hand, and somehow, there was a noticeable change, as she seemed to grin. The nurse brought over a bottle of formula and showed me how to hold it properly. This was human connection and love on a pure, deep level—placing my worldly striving and medical education in a human context. Those moments had a profound and transformative effect. I returned to my research with renewed purpose and enthusiasm, my heart and mind in balance.

Seeking more heart experience, I volunteered at a soup kitchen that served food to a line of hungry, mostly unhoused people. Intellectually, I had understood there were people less fortunate and in need of a helping hand, but seeing and experiencing this directly was a lesson in humility. While serving food, I used my heart to connect to everyone standing in line waiting for a warm meal. Shame came over me, for my comparatively privileged existence, and I was saddened and angry that not everyone had their basic needs met, especially in the wealthiest country in the world.

After my life on Wall Street, these were eye-opening and humbling encounters. Through my volunteering, I learned the importance of human heart-to-heart connection, and the value of love. I realized we are all fellow travelers in the same boat in the vast ocean of life, all needing to give and receive compassion and love. As I balanced my mind with my heart, the human element that was previously missing changed my outlook on life. I was more optimistic, and through my engagement with reality, my research took on a more profound meaning.

Giving back to the community through volunteering is crucial for one's personal and spiritual growth. By shifting the focus from oneself to others, we comprehend human suffering on a deeper level than the purely intellectual; we develop compassion and love. Loving oneself is important, but it can become selfish if excessive or exclusive. Volunteering has been one of the most fulfilling and transformative spiritual experiences in my life, and I teach this to all my students.

After about five years of demanding work and many lessons along the way, I successfully defended my thesis and was awarded a doctorate degree. In the end, my graduate program instilled valuable lessons into formulating and conducting novel experimental research—from conception to implementation. I also gained character strengths, heart-mind synthesis, and insights into the role of leadership that guide me to this day. Most important, my training gave me the sense of purpose and meaning I had hoped for.

THE FELLOWSHIP

Having earned my doctorate, I needed a position in a laboratory for postgraduate fellowship training—a prerequisite to becoming an independent researcher. Indeed, mastering science takes an awfully long time—and one is never quite done.

Serendipitously, an opportunity presented itself only weeks before my thesis defense. I attended a seminar given by a well-known HIV virologist from Columbia University whose studies on the molecular mechanisms of HIV infection in the brains of patients—the so-called Neuro-AIDS—fascinated me. During the seminar, I realized that additional training in molecular biology would round off my expertise in HIV research.

Although riddled with anxiety about asking potentially naive questions, I engaged in a conversation with the speaker, which proved intellectually stimulating for us both. Our discussion continued after the seminar, and—now fully confident, with restored ambition to move forward—I asked about a possible position in his research group. He invited me to his laboratory to give a seminar on my doctoral research on newly identified cellular mechanisms of HIV inhibition. This was my invitation for a "job interview," and I was pumped.

My talk was well received, and soon after, I was offered a postdoctoral fellowship in his molecular virology lab—which I happily accepted. Later, I realized that being present at that seminar and meeting with the speaker was another moment of synchronicity, and once again my destiny was unfolding.

The laboratory was completely different from my graduate school environment, where I labored without much support and had to figure out most of the science on my own. However, that is the purpose of graduate studies: to instill confidence and prepare students for simultaneously collaborative and competitive situations. The new laboratory was large, staffed with postgraduate fellows from all over the world, with sizeable technical support and sufficient funding for the research. It was a collegial environment with many opportunities, and once again, I was eager to learn.

Unlike being a student, there was no need to clamor for good grades or defend my thesis, and no deadlines to meet. For the first time in my career, I had the necessary support to make an impact with my research! I felt free and optimistic as my new mentor welcomed my ideas and interests. As a result, I decided to focus the research project on elucidating the molecular mechanisms by which HIV penetrates and damages specific brain cells of AIDS patients.

I made friends with people in the lab, in addition to the amicable relationship with my new advisor. I was eager to seize each opportunity to learn all I could and ended up spending long hours and weekends on my project. I was happy and content for a reasonable period of time—a rare occurrence indeed.

Success came quickly, and I published my first manuscript: "*Isolation and long-term culture of primary ocular human immunodeficiency virus type 1 isolates in primary astrocytes.*" My advisor was somewhat surprised by the quick results but pleased with my enthusiasm and work ethic. Some of my colleagues, not so much. They complained I was making them look bad in comparison, and asked me to slow down, but I was hungry and on fire. Nothing could stop me.

Soon, I realized I could accomplish only so much with my two hands. I also wanted to give back some of the extraordinary help I received along the way at Hunter and Cornell. With my advisor's approval, I contacted the biology department at Hunter College and offered to serve as a supervisor to students who would like to volunteer in the lab. This would be my first attempt at mentorship.

Not long after, Maya, an undergraduate student, came to volunteer. She was an immigrant from Indonesia, eager to learn, and excited to have this opportunity to train in an actual biomedical research lab. She worked hard and put in long hours. I was delighted to be her mentor and teach her the technical and safety protocols for the experiments. Her attitude was reminiscent of my tenure at Cornell, with all the eagerness and ambition to learn and succeed.

As a mentor, I emphasized the importance of volunteering and the use of the heart to balance the intellect. I shared my lessons learned from volunteering in the soup kitchen and in the babies' ward at the hospital. Maya was receptive to my guidance, and being a piano player, she volunteered her time at the hospital, playing for the patients. In the end, she earned an authorship on an important manuscript, as well as excellent recommendation letters from me and my mentor. Maya went on to study at a prestigious medical school and later became a physician specializing in pediatric medicine. This represented a full circle for me, as I was able to mentor and be of service in my chosen profession, paying forward all the help that had been so generously given to me.

The laboratory was across from Roosevelt Hospital on 58th Street, between Ninth and Tenth Avenues in Manhattan. There was a cozy Greek diner on the corner where I would drop by for a late supper before going home. Greek diners in the city are ubiquitous and serve just about anything you want to eat. Late evenings on the way home was the time for me to relax and enjoy my usual hanger steak, occasionally accompanied by a spicy Bloody Mary—a relaxing and happy way to end a busy and productive day in the lab.

I commuted to and from the lab by a hospital jitney bus—from my Columbia-subsidized apartment on 113th Street, across from St. Luke's Hospital and a block away from the Columbia University campus. Morningside Heights was a great neighborhood with lots of inexpensive restaurants and many students from the university. There were multicultural events and talks on the campus I would attend on weekends. The subsidized one-bedroom apartment was tiny, but comfortable, and it overlooked the splendid St. John Cathedral.

Life was good; I was content—especially with my fledgling science career. There were no worries to be had, no exams to pass, no money troubles to speak of—and I was investigating some of the most pressing questions of virology and healthcare, publishing new and exciting research results that were well received by the scientific community. It was an excellent progression from my student days at Rutgers, as now, for the first time, I was experimenting with HIV infection in medically relevant human cells, producing meaningful results that could impact people's health.

Part 3

TRANSFORMATION

This is no way for anyone who wears
white garments lightly. This is no easy stairway
I speak of here; this path is steep at first.

DANTE (PURGATORY, CANTO X, 121-123)

TRANSITIONS

Looking back, these were some of the best times in my career until—without warning—my own health took a turn for the worse: out of nowhere, I developed severe allergies and suffered daily headaches. On many days, the lab seemed like the only safe place to be—behind the thick walls of the medical research building, with the filtered air and sealed, double-glazed windows. A specialist prescribed a powerful medication that provided temporary respite. Unfortunately, the symptoms returned with vengeance as soon as the effect of the drug wore off. I could not find relief.

Then a colleague suggested I visit the acupuncturist and herbalist he saw, Dr. Yu, who had helped him with similar problems. Dr. Yu's office was conveniently tucked around the corner on 57th Street, a short walk from the lab. The doctor was an older, amicable Chinese gentleman with a medical degree who was an expert in acupuncture and herbology. He was well-known and respected and had even been interviewed on CNN about traditional Chinese healing methods.

I started acupuncture treatment with Dr. Yu, which provided only moderate relief. After several visits, he suggested another approach to treating my allergic reactions using medicinal plants or, as we would call them nowadays, natural products. By definition, natural products are derived from living organisms: algae, plants, fungi, microbial- or animal-derived extracts. I found this approach interesting, as I had read about the history of drug discovery from medicinal plants. For example, aspirin—the most widely used drug worldwide—has its origins from the bark willow tree and was used as far back as ancient Egypt. Similarly, penicillin was first derived from the fungus Penicillium, grown on decaying organic matter, and the widely used cholesterol-lowering statins were discovered in fungal species as well.

Natural products have long been an integral part of Traditional Chinese Medicine (TCM) as well as the Ayurveda system of traditional Indian medicine. Only relatively recently, searching for new compounds to combat emerging illnesses, has the Western pharmaceutical industry begun a systematic study of the medicinal properties of natural products; active research in some Western European countries is ongoing, but alas, not so much in North America.

Dr. Yu's apothecary, adjacent to his office, contained thousands of products from multitudinous natural sources—all labeled and stored—including plants, roots, tree bark, seaweeds, and many more. Dr. Yu explained their utility in treating my symptoms, but it was beyond my knowledge base, and I had no idea what he was talking about. Nonetheless, I trusted his expertise. He combined several dried plants, carefully weighing the proportions, and gave me the mixture in a paper bag with precise instructions for its preparation.

I was to boil the dried herbs in a large pot until the liquid was reduced to two cups, then drink the dark brown concoction each morning and night. The reduction took a long time and had a pungent smell that permeated the apartment (and possibly the entire building) as well as an unpleasant taste. However, after three days of drinking this brew, my symptoms improved. I returned to Dr. Yu, who, happy with the progress, continued the treatment by tweaking the composition of his concoction and sending me off with my new weekly dose of natural remedy. The boiling part remained tricky—especially when one lives in an apartment building shared with people who do not necessarily appreciate the lingering stench—but the taste could be improved by adding a spoonful of honey. I felt so much better after just a few weeks that I stopped taking my allopathic medicine altogether and remained symptom-free for a long time afterward.

As a scientist, I found this a fascinating practical experiment! Certain natural products had a remarkable and direct impact on my health, and this intrigued me. Later on, at a critical time, this memory would bubble up in my conscious mind and significantly impact the direction of my research career.

Being symptom-free and happy for it, I returned to my somewhat neglected research with renewed enthusiasm. As a postdoctoral scientist, I enjoyed the intellectual freedom I so craved but drew my salary from my mentor's funded research projects and was therefore subject to the uncertainties inherent in grant-subsidized research. So, I reasoned, if I wanted stability and to become an independent scientist with my own lab, I had to act. Postdoctoral contracts are typically renewed yearly and can terminate anytime the funding runs out. This led to researchers continuously coming and going. Some of my colleagues moved to positions in the pharmaceutical industry—which offered higher salaries and more structured opportunities for professional advancement. The way I saw it, though, the tempting financial benefits meant working on projects narrowly defined by the company and often changing based on market needs and short-term profitability.

So, after three years on this level of Purgatory, it was time to move on. I didn't want to remain a postdoc forever. My ambition was to become an independent biomedical researcher, to generate and test my ideas in a lab of my own—an intellectual sandbox to play in, so to speak.

My advisor and his continuous success in expanding knowledge in the field of antiviral research served as an inspiration for me to try an emulate him, to dare step toward achieving independent scientific status. Securing funding is a prerequisite for breaking into the academic world, and securing a faculty position in an academic institution is a prerequisite for obtaining one's own laboratory space. It is a challenging task, especially for new investigators breaking into the grant-funding game for the first time.

To compete for funding, I chose the well-established route of writing and submitting a proposal for a unique research project, an award reserved specifically for early-stage investigators. This required developing an original hypothesis and generating experimental results to support the idea. If a hypothesis is intellectually sound and novel, money can follow. At that time, a prominent direction in HIV research was trying to decipher the intricate mechanisms of infection, making slow but consistent advancements toward eventual treatment to block the virus from entering into the cells of the patient.

Science progresses methodically, like constructing a wall, one brick at a time, layer over layer, producing incremental results toward new treatments. But every so often, discoveries come in leaps, changing the course of our thinking to bring a new paradigm into existence. This process is similar to that of a spiritual practice, with long and at times frustrating periods of silence, interspersed with occasional insights of exceptional wisdom. The spiritual mountain is steep, and scaling it requires persistence, as well as patience, for watershed moments to manifest. This led me to wait and hope for the next moment of inspiration to drop into my consciousness.

I wasn't thinking along any grandiose lines, but I wanted a direction for my future independent research that would be promising and original. Ideally, something direct and immediate toward eradication of the AIDS virus. Something that would feed my intellect and excite my imagination. I felt I had it in me and just had to dig deeper within to find that singular creative idea.

This powerful motivation propelled me forward. Maybe it was mere arrogance, or my ego, but it didn't feel that way. Instead, it was as if my very destiny awaited me, beckoning me to fulfill it.

I spent considerable time reading the latest research papers, racking my brain—but there was nothing there! I kept coming up empty and frustrated. I couldn't envision an original idea, couldn't produce any attractive and scientifically viable research hypotheses that would spark my imagination and ambition. I was lacking inspiration.

This was an essential moment of transition, when one keeps making the right moves but repeatedly comes up empty. It is often tempting to just give up and settle. Yet it inspired me to work harder—to continue to think, read, and meditate. Lacking creative inspiration, it seemed that was all I had left. I questioned my abilities. Was I who I thought I was, who I wanted to be? What kind of a scientist was I, with zero original ideas? How would I succeed?

THE SPARK

Scientists throughout history have received inspiration and intuitive knowledge in various forms. Did it descend through their higher selves, through their Beatrice? The celebrated French scientist Louis Pasteur famously said, "In the fields of observation, chance favors only the prepared mind." He demonstrated the principles of vaccination and invented the eponymous pasteurization process—both of which have saved countless lives.

The visionary chemist August Kekulé, in nineteenth-century Germany, attempted to solve the elusive structure of the benzene. This long-known chemical compound baffled scientists because its chemical properties were that of a saturated carbon chain, whereas its mass suggested it was an unsaturated one. It was a truly self-contradicting chemical! After many other chemists worked on it, and failed, Kekulé had a vision in a dream, a vision of a snake biting its tail (*Illustration 3*).

He woke up with the insight that the benzene is a closed hexagon molecule, a ring—at a time when circular chemical structures were unknown. Today, the hexagonal benzene ring is an instantly recognized chemistry symbol—but in Kekulé's day, the idea of a circular molecule was groundbreaking! After debate and argument, the scientific community concurred and accepted the discovery. Kekulé's visionary breakthrough laid the basis for most of modern chemistry, championing visual scientific creativity, and his dream became an oft-cited example of the role of symbolism in creative thought.

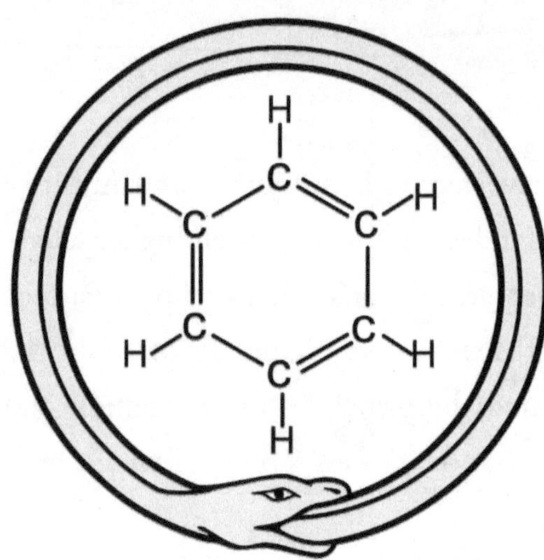

Illustration 3. Representation of the snake biting its tail that led Kekulé to envision the hexagon structure of the benzine ring.[iv]

Another example of a groundbreaking scientific insight also took place in the nineteenth century. Fifty-six chemical atoms were known at that time, each with an atomic mass slightly larger than the one before—but grouping them into underlying principles and sets with equivalent properties eluded chemists. Dmitri Mendeleev, in Russia, was also beating his head against the wall, trying to organize the chemical elements. He saw them in his mind, each endowed with its unique properties, but couldn't understand the links between them, the underlying logic.

After considerable time spent in fruitless thinking, he grew exhausted.

---

iv Ouroboros-benzene, *Wikimedia Commons*, August 1, 2023, accessed July 4, 2025, https://commons.wikimedia.org/w/index.php?title=File:Ouroboros-benzene.svg&oldid=788998198.

While napping, he saw a table of periodicity unfolding, with all the elements correctly grouped (*Illustration 4*).

Періодическая система элементовъ по группамъ и рядамъ.

Ряды	ГРУППЫ ЭЛЕМЕНТОВЪ: 0	I	II	III	IV	V	VI	VII	VIII
0	x	—	—	—	—	—	—	—	
1	y	Водородъ. H 1,008	—	—	—	—	—	—	
2	Гелій. He 4,0	Литій. Li 7,03	Бериллій. Be 9,1	Боръ. B 11,0	Углеродъ. C 12,0	Азотъ. N 14,01	Кислородъ. O 16,00	Фторъ. F 19,0	
3	Неонъ. Ne 19,9	Натрій. Na 23,05	Магній. Mg 24,36	Алюминій. Al 27,1	Кремній. Si 28,2	Фосфоръ. P 31,0	Сѣра. S 32,06	Хлоръ Cl 35,45	
4	Аргонъ. Ar 38	Калій. K 39,15	Кальцій. Ca 40,1	Скандій. Sc 44,1	Титанъ. Ti 48.1	Ванадій. V 51,2	Хромъ. Cr 52,1	Марганецъ. Mn 55,0	Желѣзо. Fe 55,9 Кобальтъ. Co 59 Никкель. Ni 59 (
5		Мѣдь. Cu 63,6	Цинкъ. Zn 65,4	Галлій. Ga 70,0	Германій. Ge 72,5	Мышьякъ. As 75	Селенъ. Se 79,2	Бромъ. Br 79,95	
6	Криптонъ. Kr 81,8	Рубидій. Rb 85,5	Стронцій. Sr 87,6	Иттрій. Y 89,0	Цирконій. Zr 90,6	Ніобій. Nb 94,0	Молибденъ. Mo 96,0	—	Рутеній. Ru 101,7 Родій Rh 103,0 Палладій. Pd 106,5 (
7		Серебро. Ag 107,93	Кадмій. Cd 112,4	Индій. Jn 115,0	Олово. Sn 119,0	Сурьма. Sb 120,2	Теллуръ. Te 127	Іодъ. J 127	
8	Ксенонъ. Xe 128	Цезій. Cs 132,9	Барій. Ba 137,4	Лантанъ. La 138,9	Церій. Ce 140,2	—	—	—	— — —
9		—	—	—	—	—	—	—	
10	—	—	—	Иттербій. Yb 173	—	Танталъ. Ta 183	Вольфрамъ. W 184	—	Осмій. Os 191 Иридій. Jr 193 Платина. Pt 194,8 (
11		Золото. Au 197,2	Ртуть. Hg 200,0	Талій. Tl 204,1	Свинецъ. Pb 206,9	Висмутъ. Bi 208,5	—	—	

Illustration 4. The Table of Elements as envisioned by Mendeleev in a dream.[v]

Mendeleev snapped out of his dream and hastened back to work. A. A. Inostrantsev's memoirs recount Mendeleev's statement, "I clearly see in a dream a table where the elements are arranged as they should be.

v Mendelejeff: Die periodische Gesetzmäßigkeit der Elemente. In: Annalen der Chemie und Pharmacie. VIII. Supplementband 1871, S. 133–229

I awoke and immediately jotted it down on a scrap of paper."[2] That was how the periodic chemical table, which we all learn in school today, came to be. Mendeleev's initial idea has been expanded with all newly discovered atoms being added to their proper place in the table. In 1906, Mendeleev was nominated for the Nobel Prize for his visionary discovery.

I certainly wasn't comparing myself to these venerated scientists but rather was hoping for a spark of creativity akin to my bookstore and the biology lecture *Aha!* moments of inspiration, which had both changed my life's trajectory and aligned me with my destiny.

After much time spent thinking—and meditating on it—hoping for that singular original spark to emerge, it arrived one day in a most unexpected way. While bouncing on the jitney from my apartment to the lab one morning—distractedly daydreaming, gazing at the life passing by on Columbus Avenue—a thought dropped into my awareness, seemingly out of the blue: *What about Dr. Yu's natural products? Could they act against viral illnesses?* I was jolted out of my daze with new excitement. I could feel familiar energy tingling in my body, and life around me went silent and faded from view. A flash of inspiration struck, and I was on fire with this new idea. This was yet another exceptional moment of synchronicity, between two distinct but related events coming together at the right moment. A new door had opened, and destiny found me again.

Since I had personally benefitted from the healing effect of Dr. Yu's medicinal herbs, it occurred to me that these extracts might inhibit HIV and slow down the progression of the AIDS blight. This was a long shot, perhaps, yet a logical assumption—and it appealed to my intellect and creativity. Finally, maybe a new idea worth testing.

I recognized that flash of inspiration by its now-familiar energy. It was like the previous moments of wisdom that had entered my awareness, but this realization had not come out of nowhere; it wasn't just good luck or chance. Instead, it was the result of my relentless work in the lab, as well as a consistent spiritual practice: daily efforts to connect with the energies of my higher mind and my heart—my Beatrice. It was chance favoring my prepared mind. By striving to live in my higher self, my heart-mind synthesis, I gained greater self-awareness and the ability to connect the dots, even when they weren't obvious.

Now it was time to put this new hypothesis to the test. In consultation with Dr. Yu, and with extensive research of TCM literature, I identified several medicinal plants whose properties suggested they might inhibit HIV infection. I returned to the lab with renewed vigor, starting to validate my hypothesis. Experiments were meticulously designed, executed with utmost care and precision. Experimental human cell lines were grown in Petri dishes, and treated with material extracted from the medicinal plants. Then, I'd introduce HIV, and impatiently wait for the results. If all goes well, some of the medicinal plants' extracts will prevent the virus from infecting the cells.

Soon enough, I started second-guessing myself about the experimental design and everything else that could go wrong. This was a nerve-racking experience filled with anticipation. Finally, it was time to collect the cells and evaluate the results. The moment of truth was here. The initial experimental results looked promising, as we observed that the plant extracts inhibited HIV infection in cultured human cells. This was a joyous moment for me personally, but also collectively, as it held a promise toward easing AIDS infection. My path forward as an independent research scientist was finally clear.

With enough preliminary data, I applied for funding. My grant application was received with favorable reviews, and after a couple of revisions and resubmissions, I was awarded considerable grant funding as a new investigator! This was a huge personal victory, and I was grateful to my advisor for his support and help.

My tenure as a postdoc was ending, and now, with funding in hand, I began looking for faculty positions at medical schools throughout the country. After plenty of interviews, rejections, as well as several attractive offers, I accepted a faculty position at Albany Medical College in the capital city of New York State.

MY OWN SANDBOX

My new—still empty—laboratory space, my own sandbox, was now ready for play (*Illustration 5*)! An open road with many unknown challenges, adventures, and opportunities lay ahead of me.

Illustration 5. A child playing in a sandbox.

I hired postdoctoral research scientists, and graduate students gravitated toward the lab to work on their doctoral dissertation projects.

They did most of the hands-on experimental work. After testing a large number of natural products, my team and I focused on one seaweed, *Sargassum fusiforme*, which showed the most promising results in inhibiting HIV infection in human cells[3] that are routinely infected and killed by the virus. We parsed out the individual chemical components isolated from the seaweed, and were able to demonstrate the physiological mechanisms of this inhibition, which was at the point of HIV cell entry *and* during the viral replication in the infected cells.

These results were a significant breakthrough for us, and we continued to receive private funding, as well as grants from the National Center for Complementary and Alternative Medicine. We continued with this work for years, regularly publishing our new findings in peer-reviewed journals.

Our grant applications continued to receive positive results for some time but began to meet with rejection as a multitude of breakthrough chemically synthesized medicines that prevent HIV infection and stop the spread of the virus became available. The four-times-a-day handful of tablets that gave patients nausea shrank to a one-a-day pill that prevented infection with barely any ill side effects.

This was great news for AIDS patients—the new therapeutic modalities transformed the previously deadly disease into a manageable chronic condition. However, for us it was spelling the end of the excitement and the fun of scientific discovery. As the urgent need for new medicines subsided, so did funding. Our timing was off, and more important, there was no interest in developing medicines from natural products, since these cannot be patented—and therefore would not be commercially profitable. Without funding, my tenure at Albany Medical College was slowly coming to an end.

By that time, I was well recognized for expertise in testing and isolating compounds from natural products with activity against viruses. A group of researchers from the First Affiliated Hospital of Henan University of Traditional Chinese Medicine got in touch and invited me to present our work on HIV inhibition by *Sargassum* seaweed at a series of lectures at different universities throughout China. A welcome surprise, as a new door seemed to have cracked open. They wanted to set up a collaboration and have my lab test some of their natural compounds against HIV. Already jaded by unsuccessful funding applications at home, I was pleasantly surprised when my research was received with such unfeigned enthusiasm and appreciation in China. They, in turn, were somewhat pleasantly surprised that a Western scientist would be delving into the intricacies of Traditional Chinese Medicine (TCM). I was recognized for my scientific contribution to the ongoing HIV epidemic and was even treated as a minor celebrity by my Chinese collaborators. It was a great boost for my bruised ego! Even more surprising, I was awarded a full academic professorship at the University of Traditional Chinese Medicine in Henan.

Ambition and hard work paid off in the end. Aptly, our last published manuscript was titled "Use of *Sargassum fusiforme* extract and its bioactive molecule to inhibit HIV infection: Bridging two paradigms between Eastern and Western medicine."[1] At long last, this hectic, yet tremendously productive and fulfilling period of my career felt complete.

MAY YOU LIVE IN INTERESTING TIMES

You know that "May you live in interesting times!" is said to be a curse? Well, to make things a bit more interesting, I began to develop strange symptoms: my eyesight went in and out of focus—perfectly fine in one moment, totally blurry and disorienting in the next. A string of ophthalmologists took their turn peering into my eyes with progressively complex diagnostic machinery, and went on to prescribe glasses with lenses of varying strengths—only to have my eyesight shift by the time the next set of expensive custom lenses was made. Only after I had spent a small fortune on useless glasses did one bright doctor quip, "Your eyes are connected to your brain, you know!" and sent me for an MRI scan of the head.

This is how I was diagnosed with multiple sclerosis (MS).

I received the call with the results while I was driving and nearly crashed my car. MS is an autoimmune neurological disease with a multitude of potentially debilitating symptoms. It is incurable, and the necessary medications to keep it at bay have unpleasant side effects. I had to take early retirement to deal with the illness and its manifestations. Not a pleasant transition at all. I was devastated!

After the initial shock and regaining some sense of reality, I sought help. Keith R. Edwards, MD was the director of the MS Center of Northeastern New York. He was also a prominent scientist who was testing new pharmaceutical therapies in clinical trials. He immediately put me on a stabilizing drug regimen that resolved many of the problems I was experiencing, and more importantly, went a long way to restoring my mental equilibrium. He also dispelled my fears of becoming disabled by ensuring me that the illness had been caught at an early stage in its progression, so I would not suffer its most punishing consequences. He restored my confidence and put me at ease. The pleasant part of managing my MS together with Dr. Edwards was that he respected my scientific knowledge and opinions, and we continued to discuss and devise effective therapies.

Continued monitoring of MS included a yearly MRI scan, and after some time, we observed that there was some neuronal repair of the brain lesions characteristic of the disease. Neuroplasticity at work—a scientific fact. I felt lucky and was thankful. Death wasn't quite imminent...yet!

Now officially retired, and relatively symptom-free, I wasn't ready to sit around and do nothing. Yet, for the first time in my life, there was, in fact, nothing to do. All I was doing was managing my MS symptoms, and after a while, this too started to feel like a waste of time as there was nothing I could do but read about the latest research and treatment options. I realized I had to let go of the need to control the disease apart from the prescribed drug regimen, and to allow my destiny to unfold on its own: another lesson learned, but a tough one.

However, this transition was truly challenging—as it is for anyone facing serious illness and suddenly unmoored from their life's mission.

I took solace in Viktor Frankl's words from *Man's Search for Meaning*: "When we are no longer able to change a situation, we are challenged to change ourselves."

Throughout this discombobulating period, I held onto and expanded my spiritual practice. The routine of teaching students and holding classes helped everything else fall into place. Remembering my past volunteer experience (and now with extra free time on my hands), I volunteered for the Junior Achievement program, mentoring local first graders and high school students. Once again, volunteer work gave me a renewed sense of purpose and joy, as well as fulfillment.

Still, deep inside, I knew nothing would last forever and things change (which is the Buddhist concept of impermanence), and that we all need to adapt to new circumstances. The nature of Nature itself is such. Our lives comprise a continuous stream of finite moments, each giving way to the next, each offering new lessons and opportunities. It's a never-ending process of living, learning, dying, and again, living. I strive to accept this reality of each moment, and to find inner peace and equilibrium through my practice. By now, with my inner wisdom integrated into my soul—at least to a greater extent—I was somewhat used to change and impermanence. In some ways, I even welcomed it, knowing that where there was more to learn, there was more to appreciate.

Part 4

THE KNOWLEDGE

Science & Spirit

As the geometer who tries so hard
to square the circle, but cannot discover,
think as he may, the principle involved...

DANTE (*PARADISE*, CANTO XXXIII, 133-135)

THE HIGHER SELF CONCEPTUALIZED

The stages of the Pilgrim's mountain climb are a roadmap for the journey to be traveled by the seeker, toward the ultimate destination of integration with the energies of the higher self, one's own Beatrice.

Over several decades of study and experimentation, I had come to understand the higher self as a vessel that holds three distinct energies: the energy of the higher mind; the energy of the heart center; and our genetic potential encoded in DNA, the workings of which are grounded in scientific thought (*Illustration 6*). In this context, the higher self is at the center of our spiritual being—the nucleus of Self. Intuition and synchronicity in this context are peripheral energies that optimize its function. Our higher self is our innate wisdom and inner knowing, and activating it—turning it on—in our consciousness can lead us out of the Hell and Purgatory of mundane existence.

The practice of meditation is the glue that holds all these energies together.

DNA is the seed of our spirit that is embedded in our genetic code, the primary spark of fire that *a priori* made us human and gives us the impetus for awakening that is our birthright. This as-yet dormant fire sits

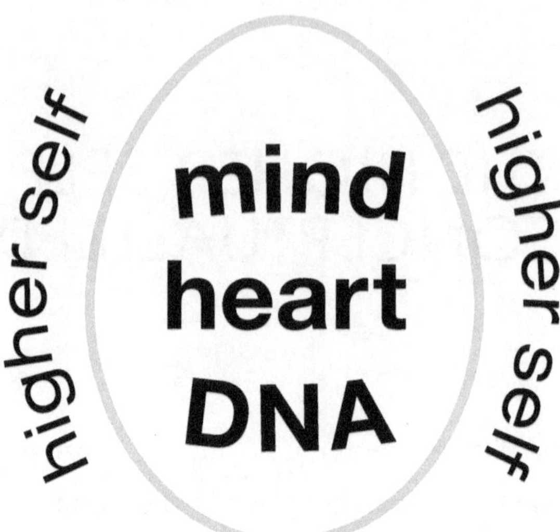

Illustration 6. Depiction of the higher self as a vessel holding together the energies of the higher self, the DNA, the heart, and the higher mind.

at the base of the higher self and is ignited by intention and our desire toward the spiritual. As an example, in my twenties, I read and searched until one day I discovered meditation and my path opened. This was not by chance, but rather because of my desire for that moment of awakening.

The **higher mind**, or the wisdom mind, is independent from the physical functions of the brain. It uses intellect but is not controlled by it. It is linked to the higher self and derives energy from it. In Buddhist thought, as explained by the Dalai Lama, the higher mind is the seed of consciousness itself.[4] The mind is connected to the heart and can transmit messages to the heart center. The mind has the capacity to bring down to our awareness the higher knowledge that exists in the alpha wave frequency, which is in the space all around us, a frequency that is amplified during meditation. For example, Mendeleev's and Kekulé's visionary discoveries. A personal example was the moment I realized the possibilities of natural products to fight or slow HIV infection. This creative moment dropped down into my awareness, but only because my mind was prepared.

When I talk about the **heart**, it is not the physical organ I refer to, but rather the heart center or chakra, which in Sanskrit means energy points of the physical body located in the middle of the chest. The heart and the mind are the principal working energies of our higher self. These energies are distinct, although they function in unison. The heart's energy is warm, and the energy of the mind is cooler. The goal is the synthesis of the heart and the mind that results in a synergistic, balanced expression of the two. My own experience of heart-mind synthesis came to me when I had to choose between two different labs for my dissertation project at the beginning of my graduate school studies. By initially working separately with the mind and then the heart, I learned the difference between the two distinct energies, and how they coalesce into the expression of balanced synthesis. Only then was I able to make the best choice.

Through our mind, we perceive knowledge, while our heart helps us experience the exhilaration and beauty of the discovery. When integrated, these two centers operate with discernment, allowing us to simultaneously experience and comprehend reality in a way that is separate from rational, intellectual, or wishful emotional thinking.

The synthesis of the heart and the mind has been recognized by contemporary scientific thought. Neurocardiology experiments have been conducted to investigate the perception of information by the heart, separate from its perception by the conscious mind.[5] The results of these experiments have shown that meditation can heighten heart perception, and, most importantly, the heart will respond to external stimulus before it has been even recognized by the brain.[5] In yet another study, it was shown that the alpha waves of the brain correlate with the rhythm of the heart, indicating the synchronous relationship between the heart and the mind.[6] In this context, the mind operates in unison with the heart, and through diligent practice, the two energies balance each other to achieve heart-mind synthesis and synergy.

Intuition is also part of our higher self, but it is a more sudden inner knowing that gives us the sensation of certainty without questioning, of understanding without doubt. It is a state from which we function via our sense of truth followed by right action.

"It is by logic that we prove, but by intuition that we discover."

—Henri Poincaré, *Science and Method* (1908)

In fact, scientific experiments in humans have shown that intuitive effects can predict future events not previously encountered.[7] This energy comes from deep within, filling us with confidence that is beyond any personal desire. This type of inner knowing is different than relying on an impulse or a gut feeling, which arise from emotions, desires, or attachments that are part of our lower ego. An impulse doesn't quite convince us, and is often followed by yet another, different gut feeling or thought arising—instilling uncertainty and doubt. On the other hand, when integrated with our heart and mind, intuition provides certainty and knowledge that is beyond doubt.

Awareness of **synchronicity** significantly advances our development, as it helps us to notice and integrate meaningful events that open doors pointing to new directions and opportunities in our lives.

"Synchronicity takes the coincidence of events in space and time as meaning something more than mere chance, namely, a peculiar interdependence of objective events among themselves as well as with the subjective states of the observer."

—Carl Jung, *Synchronicity: An Acausal Connecting Principle*

Carl G. Jung, MD, the Swiss psychiatrist, coined the term "synchronicity" to describe two separate events connected at a meaningful level of consciousness.[8] An event appears in one's mind, followed by a seemingly distinct—yet aligned—event in the physical world. It is a connection existing in two parallel realities, which becomes apparent at the level of self-awareness. It is an inner perception of certain events that later manifest in physical realization.

The more I became aware of my own dual nature—mundane and spiritual—the more I recognized synchronistic events occurring in my life. To possess awareness means to be open to possibilities that are always present around us.

My first instance of being aware of the phenomenon of synchronicity was when I was browsing the shelves of a bookstore and overcome by the recollection of an earlier meditation of mine. In that moment, I'd seen myself doing exactly that! I spotted the magazine on medical imaging, which inspired me to combine my professional aspirations as a photographer with my passion for science. The synchronistic link was that my meditation alerted me to the significance of the moment to come. In that instance, my inner and outer life aligned. Doors opened, and the right direction and opportunities presented themselves.

Our inner perception may appear through different channels, such as in meditation, in dreams, or hearing and seeing with our inner (non-physical) senses. A complete immersion in the matter we seek to understand is a prerequisite for this perception. With the sense of awareness comes the mental intention of the seeker that prepares them for the realization of synchronistic events.

A sense of **discernment** is required to determine the validity and relevance of the connection between such seemingly unrelated events, and this occurs at the level of rational thinking. Again, some doors will open, while others will close. What is relevant and meaningful in one's life can be discerned by using the technique of mind-heart analysis. Synchronicity is not a wish list of our needs, desires, or fantasy. Our wishes do not come true just because we desire them. It is not Amazon's next-day delivery service. Therefore, it is essential to distinguish between the ego desires of our lower nature and the real-life opportunities that constantly present themselves and align with our destiny.

Synchronicity is not a scientifically proven phenomenon…yet. However, it does have an appealing correlation to the physical phenomenon of **quantum entanglement**—the theory that tells us that particles of the same origin, which were once connected, remain connected, even throughout time and space.

The concept of quantum entanglement is only understood in the context of quantum mechanics. Here is how it all began: Before the field of quantum mechanics was developed, the classical Newtonian physics explained how our physical world worked—from billiard balls to gravity. However, the classical physics model of the universe could not explain forces governing the smallest sub-atomic particles, such as electrons and neutrinos.

To address these problems, physicists developed theoretical quantum mechanics models, followed eventually by experimental proof, explaining what Newtonian physics could not. The first significant achievement of quantum mechanics demonstrated that subatomic physical matter, such as electrons and photons, behaves simultaneously as both waves and particles.[9] But how can this be? Matter cannot be two things at the same time...or can it? We can measure photons or waves but cannot measure both simultaneously. This counterintuitive and paradoxical phenomenon was labeled the "wave-particle duality."

Along came Werner Heisenberg (1901-1976) with his uncertainty principle, which demonstrated that only one property of one quantum object can be measured at a time. Observation itself perturbs the system. We cannot know, for example, both the position and the momentum of a photon of light at the same time. In contrast to the classic Newtonian understanding of our world, quantum physics moved the ball forward by explaining the invisible forces that govern movement of the smallest particles of matter.

In yet another great leap toward understanding the energies that govern our universe, Einstein and other theoretical physicists proposed the quantum entanglement theory, which was followed by many experimental observations. Their counterintuitive theories were verified over time, which eventually led to three physicists being awarded the 2022 Nobel Prize in Physics for experimental proof of the entanglement theory.[9]

Entanglement is the state of two particles linked to each other regardless of how far they are from one another. The quantum state of each particle is interdependent and cannot be described separately from that of the other one. What occurs for one occurs for the other. Physical properties such as position, spin, or the momentum of the two particles are correlated. When two subatomic particles are entangled, measuring one particle instantly determines the properties of the other particle, regardless of their distance. For instance, if the total spin of the two particles is zero, one particle will have a clockwise spin while the other will have a counterclockwise spin, as measured along the same axis. This results in the overall spin of the pair equaling zero. In other words, it is one very long-distance physical relationship.

Are synchronistic events part of our spiritual awareness? Do our inner life, wisdom, mind, and heart—expressed in our meditations as visions, hearing, or seeing with our inner senses—show us events that later manifest as physical events and become real possibilities? At such moments, do we notice and recognize events aligned with our destiny? Do we take the action necessary to manifest potentialities into being?

Might these observations offer a new paradigm for understanding various parts of ourselves, our relationship to each other, and to the Universe? Since particles are entangled, are we individuals also entangled with our inner perceptions, with each other, and distant cosmic forces? After all, we are biologically complex, large and small systems that are constantly communicating with one another. We are composed of large and small particles and emit electromagnetic energy waves. We are both particles and energy at the same time. Do we perceive ourselves as part of one whole and extensive system, or do we perceive ourselves as beings separate from oneness? In fact, science has shown that quantum entanglement occurs on a macroscopic level[10] as well as a subatomic level.

The entire concept of yoga—which, as you may recall, means unity or oneness among all beings—can be attributed to quantum entanglement, with its invisible net of connections holding the entire world together.

Diligent practice and integration of all aspects of the higher self brings us new awareness and the ability to choose our thoughts and actions. This practice prepares the seeker for the next stage of advancement: recognition of one's lower nature as akin to being in Hell, which is naturally followed by the realization of the need for transmuting these base tendencies in the realm of Purgatory.

WE START IN HELL

Where man's soul goes to purify itself
and become worthy to ascend to Heaven.

DANTE (PURGATORY, CANTO I, 5-6)

The Divine Comedy opens with Hell—in fact, it begins before the actual descent into it, with the viscerally familiar sensation of being lost and rudderless, which is what ultimately leads us to the path of spiritual growth. As Dante pointed out, it is only when the Pilgrim, the seeker, recognizes the characteristics or failings of his lower nature—those aspects that have led the condemned souls to Hell—that he sees a glimmer of light, which allows him to progress to the next stage of the journey, Purgatory. However, before ascending to this realm of transformation, one must recognize and acknowledge the fears that led to non-virtuous actions and prevented forward movement. Or, to succinctly interpret Dante's wisdom: Hell exists within.

Each one of us has many different failings we all can recognize and relate to, such as bouts of pride, anger, greed, envy, and laziness, to name but a few. These negative characteristics often manifest in personality traits and actions. As we start to recognize our lower nature, fear and anxiety will arise. Like a dweller in darkness shrinking from the beam of light shone on it, the lower nature fights back. The fear center of our brain, the amygdala, becomes activated, primarily because the mind is starting to explore the yet-unknown inner realms of our nature. The amygdala starts flashing fight-or-flight warning signals: *Careful! This is dangerous! Unfamiliar territory! Stop!—what are you doing?* However, this fear response is a normal physiological response to the new and yet-unknown quest the seeker is embarking upon. Or, as Pema Chödrön has it, "Fear is a natural reaction to moving closer to the truth."[11]

When we acknowledge elements of our lower nature and consciously, by using our will, decide not to heed them, we lessen their negative impact and enhance our opportunities to tap into our higher potential—our innate wisdom. Awareness of our negative patterns is the key to success at this stage: this is why we, alongside the Pilgrim, painstakingly recognize each one, and seeing our weaknesses reflected in those patterns, hope to learn from them.

After successfully wading through the Hell of recognizing negative actions and emotions, the story continues with a climb through the aspirational circles of Dante's Purgatory. This is the realm of liberation where one can free oneself from the character weaknesses and psychological fears that keep us in Hell. Becoming conscious of negative characteristics and tendencies, and choosing not to act on these impulses, is how this work begins.

ALCHEMY

Journeying in Purgatory proper, before ascending to the summit, Dante tells of the alchemy of transforming lead to gold, lower to higher:

...where the human spirit purges itself
and climbing heavenward grows worthy.

Danta (Purgatory, Canto I, 5-6)

The esoteric meaning of transmutation is not simply closing the door to the impulses of our lower nature; instead, it is the alchemy of changing the lower self to the higher self. The seeker must face all the negative impulses one by one, examine them, and consciously decide against indulging them. This is an immensely challenging task, and it is at this stage that Dante's Pilgrim begs for help, and Virgil obliges by guiding him through Purgatory.

The process and practice of transmutation of our lower nature is in its essence illustrated in the polarity model developed by the psychiatrist Roberto Assagioli.[12] Assagioli was not only Dante's compatriot, but himself a spiritual seeker, and he recognized the significance of

Dante's text as a roadmap to a complete union with one's higher self. To help the aspiring seeker understand and process different stages of the mountain climb, he developed a model of psychological theories and practices, which are detailed in his extensive writings.[13] Specifically, for the Purgatory stage of resolving our fears, he proposed the duality model: *"We are all confronted with the forces of duality: love-hate, sympathy-antipathy, optimism-pessimism."*[14] He offers a way to balance these energies, and to create a higher synthesis.

Polarity (or duality) is a universal principle in nature, and exists in various forms within each one of us. For instance, we see physical polarity in magnetism and electricity, we experience duality in pleasure and pain, depression and happiness, personal and transpersonal self, spirit and matter, and lower and higher nature.

According to Assagioli, the duality of opposite elements is never absolute. He suggested two ways of balancing and integrating them: one is the middle way of intellectual understanding, where the opposites are blended; the other is the fusion of the opposites that is the spiritual synthesis. These two methods are illustrated below:

The middle way of blending the opposites, between the heart and the mind, is intellectual understanding. However, beyond the middle way is the synthesis of the two opposites, which in this case resides in the mind-heart union expressed in higher-self synthesis, which is shown at the apex of the triangle (*Illustration 7*). This example reminds me of the process of when I had to choose between two labs during my graduate school. My first attempt was intellectual understanding of the two options, after which I used my heart and mind separately to arrive at their synthesis and the correct choice.

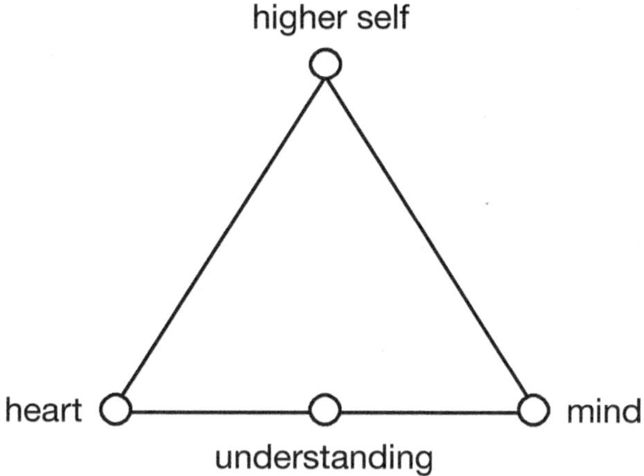

Illustration 7. The polarity model of balancing and integrating the opposites.

Pleasure-pain duality, which most of us experience at one time or another, does not imply that we should constantly seek pleasure and try to avoid pain at all costs. Fear of pain can lead to a vicious cycle of avoidance without any lasting inner peace. On the other hand, chasing pleasure can often be a temporary satisfying distraction, disguised as a pursuit of happiness. In learning to accept pleasure without craving it or becoming addicted to its pursuit, we avoid being sucked into the never-ending cycle of happiness and unhappiness. Similarly, nobody wants to experience pain, but the key is to accept the occasional physical discomfort, without fearing it. By understanding the human function of pleasure and pain, we can rise above our emotions and move toward rational acceptance of this duality.

We have achieved true long-term transformation when we no longer need to dissuade ourselves from acting out, rather than seething and waiting until the impulse to act out has dissipated. This takes time, patience, and practice, but the first step toward this worthy goal is to gain greater self-awareness and to choose to be vigilant. It is a process that becomes easier with time, mainly as we grow to recognize our inner duality and embody our infinite wisdom.

This does not mean we should repress our lower impulses, but rather transform—or transmute—those lower characteristics and find the synthesis between the opposites. If we repress our lower-nature traits, they always return—sometimes in different manifestations—to haunt us at unexpected times.

It is essential to realize that our lower nature never leaves; it is always present. We never entirely resolve it, and it never fully disappears. It is the shadow that walks next to us, and that's why self-awareness is crucial. When it arises, we recognize it but do not give it the energy of dwelling or acting on it.

"The kingdom of God is within you. Do not look for it outside yourselves. Change yourselves, and you will find that which you seek."

LEO TOLSTOY, PARAPHRASING LUKE 17:21
IN *THE KINGDOM OF GOD IS WITHIN YOU*, 1894

It is not always easy to see oneself objectively and be aware in every single moment. From my own experiences, I was lucky to have trustworthy friends whom I asked for help in pointing out my shortcomings—and they obliged. This was not easy. It was certainly difficult to hear, defensiveness was my spontaneous reaction, and the list was long. Upon reflection, though—and after a generous amount of time—I did come to recognize negative traits in my makeup and resolved to make changes. This first step, recognizing and then accepting my own negative characteristics and other limitations, was the most challenging.

Certain shortcomings on that extensive list included my being impatient, judgmental, easily dismissive, and even aggressive. I used to be very driven and intolerant of myself and others, always in a hurry to complete my tasks and add to my accomplishments. Often, when I felt challenged, wronged, or misunderstood, I acted impatiently to prove my point, arguing and even dismissing the opinions of others. I could easily lose my temper. This behavior, naturally, was not well received. Eventually, seeing myself honestly and with an open mind, I realized that being fearful and aggressive, not listening, and not valuing others' opinions was holding me back.

Deep down, I knew this was not who I wanted to be, nor did I want people to perceive me that way, so I made a conscious commitment to change. I began by intentionally *willing* myself to being present in the moment, *making an effort to pause* to gather my thoughts before speaking, and *practicing active listening*. Whenever I noticed an impulse to react—too quickly or without thinking—I willed myself to take a few seconds, staying quiet and alert, and pay attention to my emotions and impulses. I put my effort into connecting to my rational mind and analyzing the situation as dispassionately as possible. Subjected to this focused attention, the negative impulses dissipated, and I remained calm and open to listening without reacting. Gradually, my impatience diminished in intensity.

As I labored to change my negative behaviors, space opened in my mind and in my heart for positive energies to flow in. These changes were noticeable to others and resulted in more collaborations and friendships that last to this day. A double win!

This was my slow—and still incomplete—process of transformation. It's important that I point out that this process is ongoing, as negative characteristics are never fully resolved, the shadows never fully vanish. With time, they become ever subtler in nature, harder to recognize, and new ones tend to pop up. But on the positive side, my awareness of my lower nature is greater, and I can make good choices more quickly and with less effort.

Working with my students, I've noticed certain commonalities, such as the tendency to hold on to negative perceptions of self-worth. These range from a sense of not being good enough to being unwanted, unworthy, unloved, and unlovable. Such false beliefs are often rooted in childhood, arising from a general lack of love, and can cause great anguish and stand in the way of self-improvement. Since these negative beliefs are based on false perceptions, however, they can be changed through self-reflection, rational thinking, and psychological help. Understanding the origins of our negative patterns is often significant in letting go of such destructive behaviors. Once the mind understands, it can release fears and negative emotions.

Another widespread problem is the tendency toward perfectionism, which often leads to procrastination. The false belief that nothing you do is ever good enough can naturally arise from having grown up in a family that took your successes for granted but was quick to point out even innocent mistakes. It can result in endless tinkering with tasks that are never completed, or amassing degrees and certifications without ever putting them to use.

Curiously, in my scientific career, I never struggled with perfectionism—because science is objective and rational, and there is always feedback on reviewed grants and submitted manuscripts. However, while writing this manuscript, which is prose without formal structure, I found myself struggling with self-doubt, which led to perfectionism. I wrote and rewrote chapters and paragraphs, trying—and failing—to achieve a perfect flow, when one day I simply got tired of my perfectionism and realized it was time to publish the book because, otherwise, it will never reach readers. To overcome perfectionism, not only must we recognize it as a false belief, but adopt an opposite attitude. Sometimes good enough is in fact *good enough*.

The first step to overcoming negative thoughts and patterns is recognizing—repeatedly—that they are not based in present-day reality. They are part of our lower nature and need to be recognized as such. They are not *who* you think you are. Disidentifying from these feelings and emotions—mentally stepping outside the self and looking at it dispassionately—is a crucial first step in seeing ourselves objectively, and it involves breaking the negative feedback loop and not feeding into the cycle of false perceptions.

One way to do this is by looking at oneself in the mirror, taking a deep breath, and saying, "This is not who I am; it's just a feeling, a negative emotion, and I am okay." This process of disidentification—not taking things personally and looking at oneself objectively—is a vital step in breaking the cycle of the negative-thinking loop. Disidentification stops harmful and false self-identity beliefs and moves us toward positive and objective self-observation—toward recognition of our higher self.

When a friend criticized my striving as selfish and pointed out that I was only concerned with my own happiness, I explained to him that as we strive spiritually, we become more aware of unity and oneness of all matter. This consciousness changes our behaviors and the outward actions that impact the world around us. By striving toward greater integration and expression of our higher nature, we serve as a positive example for others to follow in their search for greater awareness. The result is an inclusive and positive shift in our collective human consciousness. It is important to remember that change always begins with the individual.

And so, coming out of Purgatory and now climbing toward the summit, the Pilgrim continues to ask questions, trying to understand the process. Beatrice exhortation is simple yet wise: *Anyone can do this, so stop talking and experience it! Stop fumbling around, and reach up instead to the energies of the Universe, which are all within you. Practice purposefully, directing your consciousness toward the vast Universe, making oneness possible.*

Although the sensation may be fleeting, the pursuit is transformative, leaving us deeply moved, at peace, and seeing the world as more integrated.

HOW MEDITATION CHANGES YOUR BRAINWAVES

Our brain constantly generates electrical signals in the form of energy waves with distinct frequencies. This collective electrical activity of the brain has been reproducibly measured since its first recording utilizing electroencephalography (EEG).[14,15] However, the dominant frequency wavelength our brain generates depends on our emotional state and physical activity at any given moment. Experiments measuring electrical signals in the brain of novice yoga practitioners during brief meditation have shown variation in EEG spectra, including increase in alpha and theta brain waves.[16]

The alpha waves, in the low-frequency range of 8-12 Hz, are associated with deep relaxation, gentle thoughts, and, notably, with meditative states. When you meditate, you're causing a measurable change in the way your brain operates. Alpha waves have been detected in individuals with strong spiritual beliefs and in the brains of Tibetan monks. What is most interesting is that alpha waves are present in the space all around us and at all times—this is known as the Schumann resonance effect.[17,18]

Alpha waves are part of Earth's electromagnetic field spectrum, emanating from its surface and radiating up to one mile skyward. Our everyday mental and physical existence is surrounded by space bathed in alpha waves, and when we meditate, we synchronize and potentiate our brain with alpha waves in the surrounding space.[19] Alpha is the wavelength that gives us spiritual awareness of unity—or oneness. In these rare moments of synchronous events, we can experience the oneness of life that surrounds us at all times as a physical sensation and reality. When two or more people are in sync with each other and harmoniously engaged in the same task or emotional experience (be it an intellectual brainstorming session, meditating together, or attending a concert), their brain waves become synchronized in the alpha amplitude.[20,21] This synchronization of brain waves leads to a sense of unity.[22]

In addition to the alpha waves, biofeedback brain research has shown that the theta waves, registered at frequency of 4-8 Hz, become predominant during particularly deep states of experienced meditators.[23] Theta frequencies have been shown to correlate with higher states of consciousness and the unfolding of spirituality. These deeper meditative states are associated with an area in the brain that scientists have termed the higher brain, corresponding to the higher mind of the higher self. This is a state of heightened focus, cognition, and awareness. It is the state of awareness-of-awareness itself. You are fully awake in that moment, and your experience is pure, devoid of meddling interpretations or mundane intellectual projections of the brain.

Both in deep alpha and theta states, you are in contact with your higher states of metaphysical consciousness. Thoughts, anxieties, and troubles of the day start to melt away. You may experience it as being "in the zone," the trance-like state of focused relaxation that athletes often describe as leading to their best performances. There is an absolute silence and focus, and you are one with your heart and mind. You become open to receiving images and words with the inner senses of knowing. These are deeply transformative experiences, and you perceive a sensation of silent emptiness and total freedom. It is a state of openness, grace, and humility. You are touching the energy of the spirit within, and you are one with *your* Beatrice.

THE SCIENCE OF MEDITATION

We all have the innate capacity for spiritual awakening. It is in our DNA, or, more appropriately: anyone can do this, as Dante wrote:

The heavens set your appetites in motion—
I say not all of them, but even if I did,
light is given you to know good from evil,
and free will, which, if it endure fatigue
in its first battlings with the heavens,
will then conquer all, if it be well nurtured.

DANTE (*PURGATORY*, CANTO XVI, 73-78)

My search started with being lost, not knowing my purpose, and my meaningless Wall Street job and general life unhappiness. That discontent of not knowing was the trigger that pushed me forward—seeking. All my insights, breakthroughs, and *Aha!* moments were not the product of magic or wishful thinking, but in fact were rooted in the modern sciences of the brain, mind, and heart.

Some of the most sophisticated and sensitive medical technologies have been used to demonstrate correlation between our brain chemistry and mystical experiences of oneness, and to map the exact regions of the brain involved in these phenomena.[vi]

Dr. Kenneth Kendler, a physician and scientist renowned for his work in epidemiology and genetics, led a major study in the 1990s examining the hereditary versus environmental factors contributing to spirituality.[24] This breakthrough study found that spirituality was determined by familial-environmental factors for 71 percent of participants, while 29 percent were hereditarily predisposed to spirituality. In other words, depending on our circumstances, we are all capable of and have innate capacity for spiritual awakening. However, specific genes or groups of genes contributing to hereditary of spirituality have not yet been identified and are still under investigation.

Many other studies have demonstrated that specific brain regions are associated with spiritual states of higher consciousness and mystical experiences of unity or oneness, all of which can be activated through the practice of meditation.[22]

Developments in neuroscience have led to exciting discoveries regarding oneness. Utilizing a single photon emission computed tomography (SPECT) camera, which detects specific neuronal activity and its precise location in the brain, Dr. Andrew Newberg[vii] performed brain

---

vi These technologies include: magnetic resonance imaging (MRI), functional MRI (fMRI), positron emission tomography (PET), single photon emission computed tomography (SPEC) scans, and electroencephalogram (EEG) scans, all of which have been used to accurately measure specific areas of the brain and the corresponding energy that is given off during meditation or other spiritual practices as described in the experimental protocols.

vii Andrew Newberg, MD is professor and director of research at the Marcus Institute of Integrative Health at Jefferson University Hospital. Dr. Newberg has published scanning experiments on meditating people, comparing these to scans of a nonmeditating group acting as a baseline reference control.[20] Typically, the neurons that form the orientation association area (OAA) of the brain receive input from our senses—especially touch, vision, and hearing—which allows us to experience a three-dimensional sense of our body. This human ability gives us the capacity to separate ourselves from the surrounding area we need to physically navigate. To do so, there is constant strong neuronal messaging between our senses and the OAA area, which keeps us straight up so that we don't crash into things and other people. Amazingly, in the meditating group (but not in the nonmeditating control group), neuronal signaling between the senses and the OAA area was markedly decreased. This decrease in signaling led feelings of physical separation to gradually diminish, allowing a sense of harmony to take over—the experience of oneness with the energy of the universe.

Think about this within the context of Dante, when he described the metaphysical union between Pilgrim with his higher self, his Beatrice, at the summit of the universe. These neuroscience experiments validate our human ability to achieve higher states of consciousness and experiences of oneness through meditation.

In yet another study, Lisa Miller, PhD[viii] used functional MRI (fMRI) in two sets of study participants to verify the existence and ex-

---

numerous research articles and eight books on brain function, brain imaging, and the study of spirituality and health.

viii Lisa Miller PhD is a researcher and professor in the clinical psychology program, and founder and director, of the Spirituality Mind Body Institute at Columbia University in New York City. She is the author of several books, including *The Awakened Brain* and the *New York Times* bestseller *The Spiritual Child* (2015).

perience of unity in the human brain. In one group, people were asked to recount experiences of stress, panic, or uncertainty. Their fMRI brain scans showed activation of the brain's region responsible for motivation, reward, action, and goal-oriented achievements. This part of the brain is associated with the daily grind of life we all experience, which is typically devoid of spirituality. The second study group was asked to provide detailed, personal accounts of being absorbed in something beyond themselves, so-called transpersonal experiences. The fMRI data for this group showed reduced activity in the neurons responsible for distinguishing between self and others, resulting in the sensation of dissolving physical boundaries and promoting feelings of unity and oneness—like the results obtained by Dr. Newberg's experiments.

Extending these studies, Dr. Miller looked for correlates between depression and spirituality. Utilizing electroencephalogram (EEG) to measure energy the brain produces, subjects with strong personal spiritual beliefs gave off the same wavelengths found in meditating monks—high amplitude alpha wavelength measuring 8-12 Hz. The same alpha wavelength was given off by depressed subjects who did not have strong spiritual beliefs but were treated with selective serotonin reuptake inhibitors (SSRI), medicine given to alleviate depression. However, when these subjects stopped taking SSRI medicine, the alpha waves disappeared. In contrast, the brains of subjects with strong spiritual beliefs who had recovered from previous bouts of depression continued to give off strong alpha waves. These results demonstrate strong correlation between spirituality and depression, demonstrating how spiritual awareness can guard against depression.[25]

In *My Stroke of Insight,* neuroanatomist and brain researcher Dr. Jill

Bolte Taylor[ix] describes her astonishing real-life event of experiencing oneness and inner peace that was unfortunately brought on by a massive brain stroke that completely inactivated the left hemisphere of her brain.[27] In her book and accompanying TED Talk, she describes the experience as feeling connected to the universal energy surrounding her, which she perceived through the consciousness of the right hemisphere of her brain. Dr. Bolte subsequently came to the realization that we are all capable of mystical or metaphysical experiences, of achieving the inner peace and oneness she experienced during her medical emergency.

Further, the experimental results by Dr. Miller validate and extend findings by Dr. Newberg and Dr. Kendler. Collectively, their experimental results have demonstrated that spirituality is not only our birthright, but it is detectable and visible in our brain function, and attainable for all through the act of meditation. Awakening our spiritual energies stimulates inner change, allowing us to experience the duality of existence coalescing into one balanced reality.

Beyond that, multiple studies by other investigators[28,20] have found that engaging in meditative practice is linked to improved mental and physical well-being and reduction in depression and anxiety.[29] Moreover, meditation practice decreases the impact of stressful events such as illness and divorce, and is also responsible for a reduction in addictive behaviors such as smoking and alcohol consumption. Meditation does not only improve our mental and physical well-being, it helps us to express our full and innate potential. Science has at last caught up

---

ix Jill Bolte Taylor, PhD is neuroanatomist, author, and public speaker. In 2008, Dr. Bolte was named by *Time Magazine* as one of the 100 most influential people in the world.

with and empirically validated mystical experiences described by sages, poets, and philosophers for millennia.

Part 5

MEETING BEATRICE

Ah, the strange feeling running through my mind
when I turned then to look at Beatrice
only to find I could not see, and she
so close to me, and we in Paradise!

DANTE (*PARADISE*, CANTO XXVI, 135-138)

MY PRACTICE

Pilgrim's relentless climb up the mountain incorporates tried-and-tested practical advice for the seeker. It represents a roadmap toward the ultimate union with the higher self, and "[t]he Love that moves the sun and the other stars." It has led me—and many others before—to connect with our innate wisdom, to successfully integrate the heart-mind energies, and to ultimately uncover purpose and meaning in our lives. On every level, this is an experiential and intimate journey. Meditation is the key to discovery and integration, and when we practice, we are purposefully directing consciousness toward our higher self and awakening inner wisdom.

Start slowly, although it is beneficial to establish a routine. In the end, only with the strength of your desire, resolve, and effort will you crack open the door to your inner wisdom. Once you step through this door, new possibilities emerge, and the ability to access higher knowledge enters your awareness.

My advice for those seeking to embark on the journey is this: Reading is an excellent source of education and a good starting point for researching different methods and practices. It will also provide a framework to interpret your future experiences. Ultimately, however, there is no substitute for practical experience. Find a community of people with a shared passion for truth and self-discovery. Humble yourself by embracing challenging situations. Learn firsthand from those who have traveled the same path, but above all, listen to your inner wisdom; it alone knows where you are destined to travel.

Dedicated quiet meditation space is a plus. Decorating it with objects representing beauty and wisdom is most beneficial, as this directs your consciousness toward the union you seek with your higher self. I have used fresh flowers, a potted plant, or a picture of nature representing beauty to me. In addition, you may use a meaningful figurine, a sacred image, or a photograph of a person who has spiritual meaning for you. I use a statue of the Buddha, which encompasses Buddhist philosophies and teachings of the Middle Way. This connects my awareness to that higher being whose energies I aspire to assimilate over time.

I find it helpful to begin with a short, centering relaxation exercise for my mind and body, which helps create favorable conditions for a deeper undertaking. For this, I use one of the self-centering exercises Dr. Richard Schaub[x] taught me during my psychosynthesis training—the spiritual psychology and therapy integrating body, mind, emotions, and spirit developed by Assagioli.

Try these exercises with your eyes closed, and, depending on your preference, use them alone or in tandem. They can also help in your daily life if you have difficulty falling asleep at night or if your brain is overactive and ruminating.

---

x Richard Schaub, PhD is the cofounder of the New York City branch of the Psychosynthesis Institute and an expert on Assagioli's writings and teachings. He is the author of books on transpersonal psychology and currently teaches Clinical Meditation and Imagery at the Huntington Meditation and Imagery Center.

Exercise 1:

Place one hand on top of the other, on your belly.

Follow your breath—notice the rising and falling of your belly.

Continue for about 30 seconds—following and noticing your breath and the rising and falling of your belly.

Exercise 2:

Say your name followed by—let go.

Example: On the in-breath, say, "Mario"; on the out-breath, say, "let go."

You may use this as a motivational chant (mantra), repeating it as needed.[30]

I also use a candle to focus my mind, set an intention, and gently shift my energy toward my heart, visualizing beauty, warmth, gratitude, and positive feelings toward myself and my inner self. The heart-mind connection used in this way allows for a more complete sensation of serenity and appreciation of the beauty of the world. In addition, the flame can be used to refocus the mind when it—inevitably—drifts off or gets carried away by irrelevant thoughts when the monkey mind interferes. As this happens, I open my eyes and gently refocus my mind, using the candle flame as a guide.

After I sense calmness of body and mind and I'm relaxed, I proceed to a fifteen-to-twenty-minute silent practice. Whatever posture works for you is fine—for example, sitting cross-legged on the floor or in a chair—as the physical form is only useful if you are comfortable.

I often direct my awareness to the space between my eyes—the so-called third eye—and aim to catch the sensation of the gentle movement of energy in that area. The third eye, or the invisible eye, is defined in Hinduism and Buddhism as the focal point of wisdom. It is commonly depicted on the forehead of a deity, especially the Hindu god Shiva. It represents intuition, insight, and higher consciousness. Slightly crossing the gaze with my eyes closed helps to center the energy into that space, which deepens my intention and focus.

Remain open to any sensations, thoughts, or insights that might arise. When your concentration wanes, take time to reflect and write down any thoughts that have come up, however inconsequential they may seem. If you have acquaintances who are on the same path, or if you have a spiritual teacher, you can discuss and analyze with them. These techniques have helped many of my students and have invariably improved their practice.

As you connect to your higher self, you will notice new sensations entering your consciousness. You may see images or hear words—not with your eyes and ears, but with your inner senses of seeing and hearing—the sensation of connecting to the higher self in a way that resonates with you. I return to the words of Roberto Assagioli, which I read when I'd begun my Agni yoga classes: *energies descend into images, and images descend into words.* Attending my first Agni yoga class, and hearing the words, *Why are you here?* is a good example of this phenomenon. When such sensations occur during your practice, you will understand their meaning.

How do you recognize that you've begun to connect with your inner wisdom—your higher self? Here are three common sensations which are indications you've established a connection: surprise, gratitude, and relief. The numinous is beyond words; however, once felt, it will remain with you for the rest of your life.

In addition to my daytime practice, I often meditate in the evening before going to sleep, when it is dark and quieter. I would be tired, and therefore, my mind would not be so preoccupied with thoughts of the day. I discovered I was less wired when tired, and it was easier to let go, to connect to my spirit, and to be open to any transpersonal experiences. At other times, I would practice with other seekers in the classes we shared. Mixing your practice between a solitary and group meditation may be beneficial. Through experimentation, you will find the way that gives you deepest focus and connection to your higher wisdom.

To be clear, most days my meditations were—and still are—unremarkable. This does not make them any less valuable. Often, even quieting the mind, staying focused, and sitting quietly is a challenge on its own. Over time, however, consistent practice and striving produces results, as it did for me. With intentional practice, you will uncover your inner potential and will experience the energies of the higher consciousness.

INTEGRATION

Assagioli taught that spiritual realization is experiencing part of yourself that is one with the energy pervading the Universe, writing, *"Having pervaded with one part of myself the whole universe, I remain."*[31] Throughout centuries, the oneness or non-duality phenomena have been documented in both Eastern and Western anecdotal and written records. In Western thought, as early as the second century AD, Marcus Aurelius (121-180 AD) described it in his *Meditations*: "Be mindful at all times of the following: the nature of the whole universe, the nature of the part that is me, the relation of the one to the other, the one so vast, the other so small. No one can ever prevent me from saying and doing what is complete conformity with the whole of which I am so small yet integral a part." (Book 2, Section IX)[32]

During the quiet between battles, this noblest of Roman Emperors was contemplating and writing about the oneness between his own self and the vast universe he could not deny being part of.

The duality of nature exists because we perceive physical objects as concrete matter. For instance, we see the chair and our physical body that sits in it as objects of distinct and separate matter. However, we cannot see the all-pervading energy that in fact holds all the matter together. Even though we perceive all matter as physically solid, its building blocks—the atoms and spinning electrons—are held together by microscopic energy interactions as demonstrated by the science of quantum mechanics and quantum entanglement. Our physical bodies are made of the same chemical elements the stars are made of. In fact, even our genetic code, our DNA, is made of stardust.

This idea of separation exists only in our minds, and this cognition alone can change our thinking and bring us closer to the realization of non-dualism and of the interconnectedness of all matter. These, and many other concepts, are eloquently expressed in the book *The Universe in a Single Atom: The Convergence of Science and Spirituality*, by the Dalai Lama. The profound awakened state of seeing our true nature is attained via the practice of meditation.

My own experience of synthesis occurred late one evening. I lit the tea candles on my shrine and settled down to meditate. Soon, I sensed a subtle presence next to my seated physical self. I opened my eyes, but the perception persisted and grew stronger. It was a strange but comforting recognition that there were two of us in the room. As I continued in silence, I posed two questions: *What does this image symbolize? What is the meaning?*

After a few minutes, I recognized that the standing Mario was a subtle expression of my higher self, and the sitting Mario was my physical body. I saw myself split into two separate energetic realities, which I recognized with my inner sense of seeing and intuitive understanding. Encountering myself this way was not uncomfortable, but rather a moment of realization as I was experiencing my own inner duality.

Next, I had a powerful desire to merge the two identities. In doing so, using my mind and will, I sensed an inner change in my physical body that I can best describe as a feeling of unity, strength, and peace. This was a profound sensation of two distinct life energies melding into one expression of oneness. The two separate Marios I saw were the two distinct energetic realities that exist simultaneously in all of us. One represents the physical and mundane, while the other exists in the alpha-wave frequency that surrounds us. This image represents the duality of nature that pervades all of life.

Moments like these bring us closer to the awareness and appreciation of oneness, which we encounter in everyday life but often fail to recognize. Although transient, these are remarkable occurrences, akin to the awareness of unity the Pilgrim experiences at the summit when he manages to integrate his physical self with his higher self—his inner Beatrice.

This was my first experience of seeing myself merging with the subtle energies of my higher self. To this day, at times, I still practice this mental visualization to strengthen that connection. The more I do, the stronger the link becomes. I also visualize this integration in everyday situations when I am stuck, or anxious, or when fear or uncertainty overcome me. It takes only an instance to mentally connect and bring your inner wisdom to the forefront of your conscious mind. This process works every time, and it helps me in the moment to snap out of whatever is blocking me, or out of any negative emotions of my lower self. I have successfully taught this technique to many of my students.

As Dante has it, we can all do this, and as you realize and practice this union, feelings of inner peace and strength replace the mundane anxieties of existential anguish and confusion, which naturally fade with time.

NOT MAGIC

The merging of the inner with the outer—my higher self with my mundane self, integrating the two into my consciousness—has allowed me rare but extraordinary glimpses of transpersonal experiences in situations entirely mundane, where touches of the mystical are least expected. Here, I offer descriptions of my own metaphysical moments of synthesis, as a promise that you, too, can achieve these transcendent states of being by following the Pilgrim's mountain climb.

Miami

On a sunny day in Miami Beach, I was taking a stroll on a walkway next to a row of apartment buildings with balconies overlooking the bay. I heard familiar music that I couldn't immediately place, but it brought a smile to my face, and it stopped me in my tracks. A voice from the balcony above shouted, "*Imagine*," and I went, "Oh yeah!"—instantly recognizing the John Lennon song from long ago. I just stood there for a few minutes, listening to the music and humming along with the lyrics: "Imagine all the people / Livin' life in peace / You may say I'm a dreamer / But I'm not the only one."

Wow! It hit me hard, because at that moment the physical reality dissolved and pure joy and happiness vibrated through my being. It was a transpersonal moment that moved me beyond self, and I felt hopeful for myself and the rest of humanity. Reflecting on that moment, I realized how joy and hope profoundly affect our state of being, and how we all need optimism to move forward in the pursuit of our dreams, ambitions, and desires—our destiny. Ever since, whenever I hear "Imagine," it brings back memories of that moment on a sunny day, of the happiness, the hope, and the joy.

This song, the words, and the music are a perfect example of the synergistic and unifying effect it had on me, on my heart and my mind. It served as a vehicle to lift my awareness to a higher state of consciousness. In a way, it was a mystical event—like being brushed by the hem of the clothing of a descended deity. In that instance, I experienced the beauty of the music through my heart and the wisdom of the words in my mind, thus creating a perfect transpersonal union. The song moved me to joy and hope that were beyond words.

Philadelphia

A different realization took place at a museum exhibit in Philadelphia, when I came across a sculpture of Saint John the Baptist by Rodin. As I stood before it, an inexplicable force held me captive, literally—I couldn't walk away. It was as if the dark polished bronze figure of the preaching saint, one arm extended as if beckoning, had magnetic properties, pulling me in. I was mesmerized, as if the metal were animated by divine presence.

I tried to close my eyes to feel its energy, but the experience was far more potent with my eyes open, and so I focused, looking at the statue as I stepped around it. Again, physical boundaries around me were dissolving, and it was a feeling beyond joy—almost a state of bliss—standing there wide awake and with my eyes wide open. After the passing of many timeless minutes, I willed myself away and on to the rest of the exhibit, but only that one sculpture, at that moment, had such a powerful effect on me.

I have no explanation as to what that was, except to say that certain objects of beauty can energetically resonate with an individual, to elicit feelings of joy and to propel us to a transpersonal mystical experience. There are multiple reported instances of people being mesmerized by religious paintings and statues, especially by the Italian master artists. So, it can happen to you too—keep your heart open.

Montreal

The most recent energetically remarkable moment was at a small, loud jazz club in Montreal. The Alex Bellegarde Latin Jazz band was playing in a tiny cellar (*Illustration 8*). It was a truly electrifying performance of improvisational jazz, and the band was in total sync—both with one another and with the audience.

Michel Cantero's vocals and his performance on the piano were astounding. His energy at the piano was so powerful that it moved me to tears. It was like I was surfing the stars without any physical boundaries standing in the way. After the performance, I expressed my gratitude to Michel multiple times, and he humbly responded with a simple "My pleasure!" acknowledging the profound effect he had had on me. This was a shared experience, too: the energy of the performance spread over the audience, tugging on everyone's heart in a truly unforgettable way. I do hope to have the opportunity to see him perform again.

Illustration 8. The Alex Bellegarde Latin Jazz band, Michel Cantero vocals and piano, and Alex Bellegarde on contrabass.

Collectively, these experiences shared energetic similarities—they had the effect of dissolving physical, mental, and emotional boundaries. In these moments, I was unaware of the space around me or even of my physical or mental self. I was not present in the conventional sense of being, as hard physical boundaries dissolved into a soft effervescent space, merging into one elevated mystical sensation of happiness and joy. In these brief transpersonal moments, there was nothing to mull over or worry about, there were no thoughts and my mind was empty, resting in peace and joy: it felt like the ultimate experience of freedom and peace. Maybe it was something similar to the sensation of oneness with the universe experienced by Jill Bolte,[26] the one described by Marcus Aurelius, or the Pilgrim's union with Beatrice.

My infrequent mystical moments were not sequential and have occurred throughout my practice over decades. However rare, they have given me the inspiration and courage to teach, to overcome obstacles, and to continue the path of integration. It has been well worth it and remains so, and I encourage you to step onto your own path of self-discovery and enlightenment.

THE PROMISE

The events described in these pages were not magical, and it is important to realize that we can all have transformative experiences, not only in meditation, but whenever we open our hearts and minds to the energy and beauty that surrounds us at all times. It is the mental intention and the practice of meditation that prepares us for such moments—where the ordinary and extraordinary merge into mystical unity. The spiritual practice of connecting to our higher self, to the heart and the mind, allows us to transcend the mundane and to experience the exceptional.

I strive to help the seeker in you achieve your moments of the extraordinary. We are all genetically predisposed to experience this.

YOUR MOMENT AWAITS YOU!

Bibliography

1. Gu Hui-Jun Guo, Yan-Ze Liu, Elena E. Paskaleva, Manoj Arra, Jeffrey S. Kennedy, Alexander Shekhtman, Mario Canki. "Use of *Sargassum fusiforme* Extract and its Bioactive Molecules to inhibit HIV Infection: Bridging Two Paradigms between Eastern and Western Medicine." Chin. Herb. Med. 6, 265-273 (2014).

2. Inostrantsev, A. A. Vospominaniia [Memoirs], p. 144. St. Petersburg: 1998, ISBN 5-85803-109-9 http://paleostratmuseum.ru/files/Inostrantsev,1998.pdf.

3. Elena E Paskaleva, Xudong Lin, Karen Duus, James J McSharry, Jean-Claude L Veille, Carol Thornber, Yanze Liu, David Yu-Wei Lee, Mario Canki. *"Sargassum fusiforme* fraction is a potent and specific inhibitor of HIV-1 fusion and reverse transcriptase." Virol. J. 5, 8 (2008).

4. Dalai Lama, D. *The Universe in a Single Atom: The Convergence of Science and Spirituality.* (Potter/Ten Speed/Harmony/Rodale, Westminster, 2005).

5. McCraty, R., Atkinson, M. & Bradley, R. T. "Electrophysiological evidence of intuition: part 1. The surprising role of the heart." J. Altern. Complement. Med. N. Y. N 10, 133–143 (2004).

6. Kim, D., Kang, S. W., Lee, K.-M., Kim, J. & Whang, M.-C. "Dynamic correlations between heart and brain rhythm during Autogenic meditation." Front. Hum. Neurosci. 7, (2013).

7. Bradley, R. T., Gillin, M., McCraty, R. & Atkinson, M. "Non-local intuition in entrepreneurs and non-entrepreneurs: results of two experiments using electrophysiological measures." Int. J. Entrep. Small Bus. 12, 343 (2011).

8. Jung, Carl. G. *Jung on Synchronicity and the Paranormal: Key Readings*. (Routledge, London, 1997).

9. Jacoby, Mitch. "Quantum entanglement takes the 2022 Nobel Prize in Physics." CEN Glob. Enterp. 100, 6–6 (2022).

10. K. C. Lee, M. R. Sprague, B. J. Sussman, J. Nunn, N. K. Langford, X.-M. Jin, T. Champion, P. Michelberger, K. F. Reim, D. England, D. Jaksch, I. A. Walmsley. "Entangling macroscopic diamonds at room temperature." Science 334, 1253–1256 (2011).

11. Pema Chödrön, *When Things Fall Apart: Heart Advice for Difficult Times* (Boston: Shambhala Publications, 1997), 1.

12. Assagioli, Roberto. *The Balancing and Synthesis of the Opposites*. (1972).

13. Assagioli, Roberto. *Psychosynthesis: A Collection of Basic Writings*. (Synthesis Center Incorporated (in cooperation with the Berkshire Center for Psychosynthesis), 2000).

14. Roberto Assagioli, "*The Balancing and Synthesis of the Opposites*," Psychosynthesis Research Foundation No. 29.

15. Berger, H. "Über das Elektrenkephalogramm des Menschen: Vierte Mitteilung." Arch. Für Psychiatr. Nervenkrankh. 97, 6–26 (1932).

16. Fox, K. C. R., Foster, B. L., Kucyi, A., Daitch, A. L. & Parvizi, J. "Intracranial Electrophysiology of the Human Default Network." Trends Cogn. Sci. 22, 307–324 (2018).

17. P. Stapleton, J. Dispenza, S. McGill, D. Sabot, M. Peach, D. Raynor. "Large effects of brief meditation intervention on EEG spectra in meditation novices." IBRO Rep. 9, 290–301 (2020).

18. *Handbook of Atmospheric Electrodynamics*. 1. (CRC Press, Boca Raton, 1995).

19. MacGorman, D. R. & Rust, W. D. *The Electrical Nature of Storms*. (Oxford University Press, New York, 1998).

20. Miller, L. *The Awakened Brain: The New Science of Spirituality and Our Quest for an Inspired Life*. (Random House, New York, 2021).

21. Newberg, A. B. *Principles of Neurotheology*. (Ashgate Pub, Farnham, Surrey, England; Burlington, VT, 2010).

22. Newberg, A. *Neurotheology: How Science Can Enlighten Us about Spirituality*. (Columbia University Press, New York, 2018).

23. Newberg, A., D'Aquili, E. & Rause, V. *Why God Won't Go Away: Brain Science and the Biology of Belief*. (Ballantine Books, New York, NY, 2002).

24. Ned Herrmann. "What is the function of the various brainwaves?" Scientific American (1997).

25. Kendler, K. S., Gardner, C. O. & Prescott, C. A. "Religion, psychopathology, and substance use and abuse; a multimeasure, genetic-epidemiologic study." Am. J. Psychiatry 154, 322-329 (1997).

26. Miller, L. *et al.* "Neuroanatomical Correlates of Religiosity and Spirituality." JAMA Psychiatry 71, 128-135 (2014).

27. Clark, D. "The 2008 TIME 100 - TIME." Time (2008).

28. Taylor, Jill Bolte, PhD. *My Stroke of Insight: A Brain Scientist's Personal Journey.* (Penguin Books, 2009).

29. Loehlin, J. C. *Genes and Environment in Personality Development.* (Sage Publications, Newbury Park, 1992).

30. Kaushik, M., Jain, A., Agarwal, P., Joshi, S. D. & Parvez, S. "Role of Yoga and Meditation as Complimentary Therapeutic Regime for Stress-Related Neuropsychiatric Disorders: Utilization of Brain Waves Activity as Novel Tool." J. Evid.-Based Integr. Med. 25, 2515690X20949451 (2020).

31. Schaub, Richard, PhD & Schaub, Bonney G. "Transpersonal Development: Cultivating the Human Resources of Peace, Wisdom, Purpose and Oneness." (Florence Press, 2013).

32. Bhagavad Gītā 10:42, quoted in "Roberto Assagioli, The Self and Self-Realization" (Florence: Institute of Psychosynthesis, 1974), 21.

33. Marcus Aurelius, Hicks, C. S. & Hicks, D. V. *The Emperor's Handbook: A New Translation of The Meditations.* (Scribner, New York, 2002).

Acknowledgments

From the very beginning of my writing adventure, I received much help and valuable advice that made me push forward through my hesitations with intention and purpose. And so, I express my gratitude to Nanette Hucknall—my teacher, confidant, and friend—who, over many years, helped me discover my own inner wisdom and step onto the path of self-discovery and teaching. To my beloved wife, Elena Paskaleva, for her unconditional love and support, and her contributions that made this narrative more accurate and fun to read. To Richard Schaub, for being generous with his time, for the conversations and the help in conceptualizing Dante and Assagioli into my teachings. To Mark Solomon for his friendship, lively discussions, creative ideas, and for always cheering me along.

Special thanks to Stephen Ringold, Thom Dean, Peter Golden, Tom Faddegon, Georgia Pettit, and to all the members of the HSY community for their help and support.

Special thanks to Lili Clendenning, who gave the manuscript its initial cohesiveness out of a stack of individual essays. And to the extraordinary editor Alice Peck and her editorial team, who made the book sparkle.

About the Author

Mario Canki, PhD arrived in the US as an adolescent and built his life and career from the ground up. After working on Wall Street, he became disillusioned and chose to dedicate himself to improving the lives of people suffering from AIDS. His deep curiosity about the intersection of science and spirituality led him to earn a doctorate in molecular virology and to study Higher Self Yoga teachings for over thirty years.

Dr. Canki also explored Psychosynthesis—a spiritual psychology and therapeutic approach developed by Roberto Assagioli, MD—and trained in Clinical Meditation and Imagery at the Huntington Meditation and Imagery Center in Huntington, New York.

Drawing inspiration from Dante's *Divine Comedy*, he has developed a model for the spiritual seeker that follows the Pilgrim's journey—from the depths of Hell to the ultimate union with the higher self, symbolized by the inner Beatrice. Today, he integrates these teachings to guide students and seekers on their own paths of self-discovery and purpose, blending intellectual understanding with spiritual growth.

Mario Canki can be reached at: www.mariocanki.com.

www.ingramcontent.com/pod-product-compliance
Lightning Source LLC
LaVergne TN
LVHW090610110826
845146LV00001B/324

* 9 7 9 8 9 9 4 0 9 8 5 0 9 *